Native Americans
The People and
How They Lived

Native Americans
The People and How They Lived

by
Eloise F. Potter
and
John B. Funderburg

Published by the
North Carolina State Museum of Natural Sciences
Raleigh, North Carolina
in Honor of
The Year of the Native American
1986

Drawings reproduced on pages 46, 47, and 58
Copyright 1964 The Trustees of
The British Museum. From
AMERICA 1585: THE COMPLETE DRAWINGS OF JOHN WHITE
edited by Paul Hulton. Copyright 1984
The University of North Carolina Press.
Used with permission of the publisher.

Photographs reproduced on pages 28 and 29
used with permission of the
Duke University Museum of Art

Copyright © 1986
North Carolina State Museum of Natural Sciences
P.O. Box 27647, Raleigh, N.C. 27611

Library of Congress Catalog Number 86-61434

ISBN 0-917134-09-5 (cloth) $18.95
ISBN 0-917134-10-9 (mylar) $14.95

James A. Graham
Commissioner of Agriculture

John B. Funderburg
Director, North Carolina State Museum
of Natural Sciences

Dedicated to

BETTY OXENDINE MANGUM

*whose pride in her heritage
and love for children inspired us
to write this book*

Publication of this book
was made possible through the
generous support of the
A. J. Fletcher Foundation

Designed, assembled, and illustrated
by associates of Ferree Studios, Inc.,
James Keith Birdsong, Patricia Gural Hinton,
Steven Solum, Elaine Selden, and
T. S. Ferree, Jr.

Contents

Acknowledgments **8**
Preface **11**
Beginnings **13**
Exploring America **19**
Settling America **23**
Native Americans in North Carolina **39**
The Algonquians **45**
The Two Roads **67**
Places to Visit in North Carolina **74**
Sources and Suggested Reading **76**
Native American Organizations **78**
Index **79**

Acknowledgments

This book was written and illustrated in cooperation with the Native American people of North Carolina.

The authors are particularly indebted to Betty Oxendine Mangum, of the Division of Indian Education, N.C. Department of Public Instruction, who consulted with us about the overall planning of the book and circulated the manuscript to knowledgeable reviewers in the Indian community.

Among the manuscript readers who offered constructive and encouraging comments were Adolph Dial, of Pembroke State University; Linda Oxendine, director of the Native American Resource Center at Pembroke; Bruce Jones, Janet Jacobs, and Danny Bell, of the N.C. Commission of Indian Affairs; Arnold Richardson, visiting artist at Durham Technical Institute; Lena Epps Brooker and Jane Smith of the Triangle Native American Society; Michelle Francis, archivist with the Episcopal Diocese of North Carolina; Mary Frances Morrow; Robert Wolk of the N.C. State Museum staff; Julie Wesson, a grade-school student; and Gladys Baker, PaulaRuth Ford-Potter, and Fred West, who offered the viewpoint of the classroom teacher.

Archaeologist David S. Phelps, of East Carolina University, made helpful suggestions, particularly regarding the Algonquian chapter. Stephen R. Claggett, Mark A. Mathis, and Billy L. Oliver, of the Archaeology Branch, Division of Archives and History, N.C. Department of Cultural Resources, provided access to artifacts and other technical assistance for the illustrators. Claggett and Mathis also reviewed the manuscript.

David Williams, of the N.C. Wildlife Resources Commission, and James Melton White, Jr., allowed the illustrators to study Indian artifacts from their private collections.

John E. Kuchnia, Department of Natural Resources and Community Development, assisted with preparation of the maps.

Danny Bell, Delane Boyer, Tim Brayboy, Lindsey Brooker, Karen Burns-Privette, Wanda Burns-Ramsey, Jacque Garneau, Darlene Jacobs, Drake Jacobs, Betty Oxendine Mangum, Arnold Richardson, Greg Richardson, Jane Smith, and Larry Townsend graciously posed for the major illustrations.

Louise Tharaud Brasher, assistant curator of the Duke University Museum of Art, granted permission for reproduction of photographs of pre-Columbian Peruvian artifacts from the museum collections. Kathryn Haywood, of The University of North Carolina Press, made arrangements for reproduction of the John White drawings, which are copyrighted by The Trustees of the British Museum.

All who have worked together to produce this book are deeply grateful to the A. J. Fletcher Foundation, which awarded the North Carolina State Museum of Natural Sciences a grant to help cover the costs of the design and printing. Frank U. Fletcher, grants coordinator for the foundation; James Fletcher Goodmon, foundation chairman; and Claire Freeman, a member of the foundation board, have shown a personal interest in the publication of *Native Americans, The People and How They Lived*. We sincerely appreciate their concern for the Indian people of this state and their support of the museum in its celebration of 1986 as the Year of the Native American in North Carolina.

Native Americans
The People and How They Lived

Preface

The People.

That is what they called themselves.
Christopher Columbus called them Indios.
Today they are known as American Indians,
Native Americans, or just plain Americans.

This is the story of the People:
their origins, their explorations,
and their accomplishments.
This is the story of the first Americans
and the first North Carolinians.

Most of all, this is a tribute to the Native
Americans who live in North Carolina today
and strive to make our state a place of
opportunity for all people.

1

Beginnings

A hundred million years ago, there were no human beings living anywhere on Earth. This was the Age of Dinosaurs, when reptiles large and small roamed the land and buried their eggs in sand or other loose soils. Their tough, scaly skin and the moisture-conserving shells on their eggs enabled the dinosaurs to leave the waterways and inhabit lands unoccupied by their predecessors, the amphibians.

Some dinosaurs developed large, many-branched, light-weight scales that enabled them to glide, and eventually fly, from place to place. These were the ancestors of modern birds. Other dinosaurs lived in the cold regions of the Earth and, unlike modern reptiles, must have had some internal means of keeping their bodies warm.

Living among the giant dinosaurs were a few small, secretive, warm-blooded animals that had fur instead of scales. Some of them bore their young alive instead of laying eggs, and the mothers nursed their babies with milk produced in mammary glands. These were the first mammals.

For reasons scientists still debate, the great reptiles and lots of other animals died out about 65 million years ago. Taking advantage of changing conditions, the insignificant little mammals began to increase in numbers and in size. By 35 million years ago, the present-day groups of mammals had become the dominant form of life on Earth. During the Ice Age (about one million to ten thousand years ago) so much water became frozen in the polar ice caps and continental ice shields that the ocean levels dropped as much as 300 feet, exposing many of the present-day continental shelves and creating a land bridge between Asia and North America. This isthmus enabled the horse and camel, which originated in North America, to cross the Bering

During the Ice Age, so much water was frozen in the polar ice caps and continental ice shields that sea levels dropped as much as 300 feet. This exposed continental shelves that are now under water and created a land bridge (isthmus) connecting Asia and Alaska where the Bering Strait is today. Paleo-Indians are believed to have walked across the Bering land bridge between 23 and 25 thousand years ago. At that time the receding glaciers had opened a route from the northern coast of Alaska southward along the eastern edge of the Rocky Mountains to the central portion of the United States. By the end of the Ice Age (about ten thousand years ago), Indian people had explored and populated nearly all of North and South America.

Strait to Asia. Wooly mammoths, mastodons, bison, musk-oxen, moose, deer (including caribou), antelope, cheetahs, lions, saber-tooth tigers, wolves, goats, big-horn sheep, and bears that evolved in Europe and Asia came to North America. Horses, llamas, giant ground sloths, and armadillos migrated to South America. These migrations took place only at times when routes to the Bering land bridge were not blocked by the ice—in places nearly two miles thick—as it slowly advanced and retreated many times during the Ice Age. At their greatest extent, the glaciers of the Wisconsin Period (115 thousand to 25 thousand years ago) in North America reached southward to the present-day valleys of the Missouri and Ohio Rivers.

Between two and three million years ago, some African mammals called hominids (man-like) had learned to walk on two feet and had begun to use stones and bones as tools. By about 300 thousand years ago the population of the earliest known *Homo sapiens*—the scientific name for human beings, which means "man, the wise or sensible"—began to increase rapidly and to develop many variations, including a much larger brain. One of the best known of these primitive men was the Neanderthal, who hunted with spears and had a brain much like that of modern man. The Neanderthals, named for a valley in Germany where their bones were discovered in 1856, lived in Europe and the Middle East during the Ice Age. Cro-Magnon Man, apparently more intelligent and more skillful in the use of tools than his predecessors, arose about 35 thousand years ago, possibly somewhere in the Middle East or Central Asia. Scientists consider him to have been the first truly modern human being. Supplementing his diet of easily gathered foods by hunting, fishing, and trapping, modern man quickly—at least quickly as geological ages go—populated Africa, Asia, and Europe, bringing with him great technological advances in arts and crafts. No one knows exactly when human beings first came to North and South America. Perhaps a few arrived 40 thousand years ago or earlier, but widespread exploration of the New World does not appear to have occurred until much later.

Between 25 and 23 thousand years ago, the receding Wisconsin ice shield reopened a land route from Asia to the central portion of the United States by way of the Bering Strait, the low-level northern coastline of Alaska, and the Mackenzie River valley of Canada. At this time the Bering land bridge probably was, as it may have been through much of the Ice Age, an open grassland warmed by currents of the Pacific Ocean and teeming with game. Archaeologists, the scientists who study the material remains of human life and reconstruct the way people lived in the past, have found few bones and tools that can be attributed to Ice Age inhabitants along the route the first Americans apparently followed to the New World. At the end of the Ice Age, rising seas flooded much of the land they crossed; inland campsites lie beneath the frozen tundra of the far north.

On the basis of what is known about other societies of hunters and gatherers, we can be sure that people did not come to the New World as a large, organized army of invaders. Over a period of more than a thousand years, following paths worn by great herds of game animals, they came in small hunting parties. These bands or clans, each comprising thirty to sixty people closely related by birth and marriage, brought with them only slightly different customs and physical traits. The total number of men and women surviving the long and perilous journey may have been fewer than five hundred. Reclosing of the ice barrier isolated these hunters from their relatives in Asia for about ten thousand years, until the end of the Ice Age.

The people who came to North America during the Ice Age were completely modern *Homo sapiens,* with full-sized brains and a spoken language, and they shared certain physical characteristics with the Mongoloid people living in Asia today. They had the distinctively curved, shovel-shaped front teeth (incisors) that appeared among East Asians about forty thousand years ago. They also had high cheekbones, wide-set dark eyes, yellowish brown skin, straight black hair, and very little hair on the face and body. However, the ancestors of the American Indians made the journey before the Mongoloids developed their characteristic eye folds and pads of fat on the cheeks. The Eskimos, who apparently did not reach Alaska until the end of the Ice Age, more closely resemble their Asian neighbors across the Bering Strait than any of the American Indian populations past or present. A major difference is that Type-B blood, which is rare among American Indians, is not rare among the Eskimos.

The first Americans—the Paleo-Indians—hunted the large Ice Age mammals and used their trails to reach places where edible plants and small game were abundant. These people may have scavenged meat from kills made by animal predators. Paleo-Indians probably relied heavily on nets, somewhat like tennis nets but much longer, for trapping rabbits and other small game. During a hunt, some people held the net extended in a semicircle while the rest drove game toward it. Nuts, seeds, and berries were gathered and probably were carried to camp in baskets, either woven from pliable plant fibers or shaped from bark.

The cool, moist weather conditions of the Ice Age created vast grasslands that supported herds of very large mammals known collectively as the Ice Age megafauna. Two of the most famous of these animals that became extinct when habitat conditions changed at the end of the Ice Age are the wooly mammoth and the American mastodon (center left). Clockwise from the mammoth are the giant deer, saber-tooth tiger, camel, short-faced bear, giant ground sloth, giant bison, horse, giant beaver, glyptodont, and wolves, which then, as now, culled the herds.

The earliest tools found in North America were crudely made. They included small grinding stones and mortars for crushing nuts and seeds, hand-held axes, scrapers, skinning knives, and drills. Spear points were made from splinters of bone or from stone flakes chipped on one face. Spear shafts were the long, slender leg bones of large mammals. No doubt the people who made these tools dressed animal skins, which they may have fastened together with sinews (animal tendons) to make clothing for protection from the cold weather of the Ice Age. They also knew how to start fires by striking flint against iron pyrite, a hard, yellowish mineral popularly called "fool's gold."

Lacking skill in pottery making and finding it impractical to carry heavy utensils from place to place, the early Native Americans cooked meat by roasting it over open fires or made stews by boiling food in pits lined with skins. The water was heated by dropping hot stones into it. Cracked boiling stones can be found at many campsites, which often were on hilltops and ridges. These sites provided places for watching the movements of the herds and also were near sources of good stone for making tools. The lowlands were occupied, too, especially where fish and shellfish were abundant.

Indians took the animals they needed, and every part was used for food, clothing, or tools. Bones were broken to reach the nutritious marrow. When meat was plentiful, the excess was dried for later use. Animal parts that were not edible were turned into clothing, blankets, tools, or ornaments. Hooves were used to make glue, and even the dung was used for fuel. With such frugal habits and the rich natural resources of two vast, sparsely populated continents open to them, these early Americans were able to survive the hardships of the Ice Age.

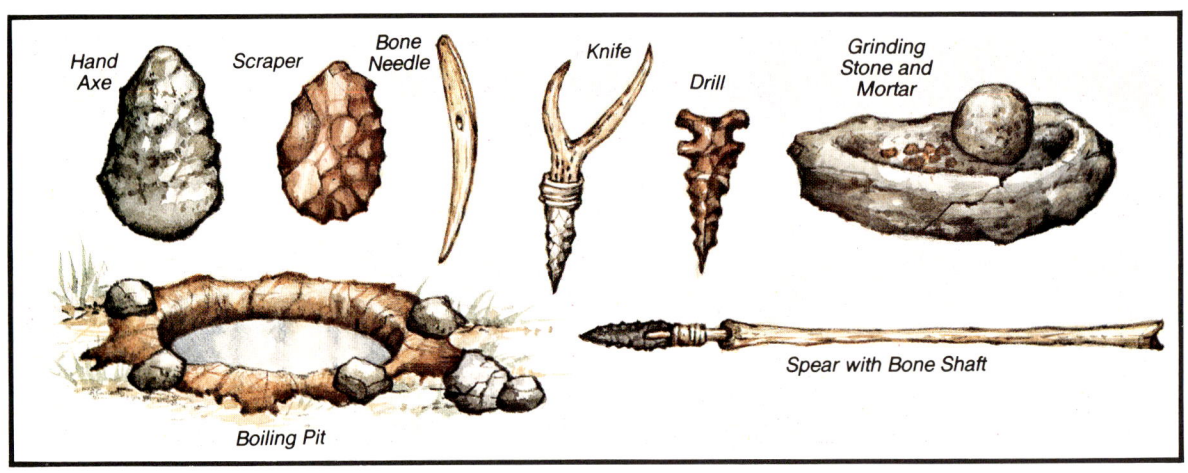

2

Exploring America

The first Americans did more than survive. They prospered. As each band increased in population, new hunting groups split off and went their separate ways. However, related bands kept in touch by occasionally hunting and feasting together, by using a common language, and by exchanging marriage partners. Thus wandering hunters could almost always find food and shelter among neighboring bands. Of course there were disputes, but most probably were settled as family matters or through competitions rather than by warfare. If differences could not be settled through peaceful discussion or if game herds dwindled, there was plenty of open land for migration to new—and perhaps better—hunting grounds.

For thousands of years descendants of the early immigrants moved southward until, having crossed a wide and grassy Isthmus of Panama and having scaled the Andes Mountains, they reached the tundra at the tip of South America—eleven thousand miles from the Bering Strait. A site about 800 miles south of Santiago, Chile, may have been occupied as early as fourteen thousand years ago. Paleo-Indians crossed the Rocky Mountains to the Pacific coast, where they established a culture based on salmon fishing. They crossed the Appalachian Mountains to the Atlantic coast. We know where they went because of their numerous temporary campsites and the tools they dropped along the way.

As distance, mountain ranges, and wide rivers separated the clans, those people who continued to intermarry began to look different from the people they left behind. Some clans became mostly tall or mostly short; others developed certain shapes for noses, chins, or foreheads. Faced with different

A Paleo-Indian hunter prepares to strike a fatal blow to a wooly mammoth that has already been weakened by jabs to vital organs such as the bladder.

living conditions, they also developed different skills, languages, and social customs. When and where two distinctive populations met, however, the technological advances of each passed to the other.

About eleven thousand years ago, some Native Americans began making large quantities of specialized spear points. Some of the oldest of these were found in a cave in the Sandia Mountains near Albuquerque, New Mexico. The Sandia point is believed to have been developed from the fluted Clovis point. Fluting consists of a groove running from the base toward the tip. Often applied to both faces, fluting simplifies attachment of the point to the shaft. Clovis points were three to five inches long and sharp enough to pierce the tough hide of a ten-ton mammoth. Named for the site in New Mexico where they were first discovered, Clovis points were scattered all over eastern North America by ten thousand years ago. They provided the first evidence of human activity in North Carolina.

Paleo-Indian hunters brought fluting to perfection in the Folsom points, which were discovered buried amid the remains of a wide-horned bison at an archeological site near Folsom, New Mexico. Made of chert, chalcedony, jasper, or petrified wood, spear points later came in several styles other than fluted: flaked in parallel ripples, stemmed, notched, triangular, or slim and tapering at both ends like a willow leaf. Long journeys were made to get just the right kind of stone, and many long hours were spent patiently flaking and chipping each point to meet the needs of the hunter. Broken spear points were reworked, creating many variations in size and shape.

Even armed with large, sharp spear points, the bold hunters probably killed an adult mammoth or bison only occasionally. The usual strategy apparently was to cut from the herd a young animal that could be driven into the mire around the water hole. There the helpless animal was killed with a carefully placed jab to the heart or spine, or perhaps dispatched quickly with a blow to the skull from a large boulder. Another tactic, probably used only when two or more bands worked together, was to stampede an entire herd over a cliff or into a dead-end canyon.

Mounted Clovis Point

Clovis Point

While the Paleo-Indian hunters were perfecting their skills, many of the animals they sought were already marked for extinction. Because large mammals such as elephants reproduce very slowly, selective hunting of the young was sure to reduce the herds drastically; but another factor actually sealed the fate of the huge Ice Age mammals. Slowly, but surely, the glaciers receded, turning lush grasslands, tree-lined streams, and shallow lakes into arid plains and deserts. Eventually, there was not enough grass to keep the herds alive. The undomesticated American camels and horses, along with the giant armadillo and many other animals, soon followed the mammoths and big-horned bison to extinction. Musk-oxen followed the receding glaciers and tundra northward. Ten thousand years ago, the buffalo still roamed the Great Plains of North America, and much later they provided a livelihood for the Plains Indians; but big-game hunting would never again be the same.

In the eastern United States, the Great Lakes region, and southern Canada, forests sprouted where there had been ice and treeless tundra. At first these forests were mostly pines and other cone-bearing evergreen trees. After many years, some of these conifers would be replaced by hardwood trees such as oaks and maples. Wind, fire, decay, and beaver ponds would create openings in the great forests and increase the abundance of small animals. Some of the people who learned to live in this changing environment and to modify it for their own benefit are known today as the Eastern Woodland Indians.

3

Settling America

From nine to ten thousand years ago, the end of the Ice Age brought worldwide changes in sea level, climate, and plant and animal life. Forced to seek new sources of food and to develop new skills for hunting in deserts and forests, Native Americans showed great ingenuity. Realizing that plant foods and small game could be found most easily in familiar territory, people began living in several semi-permanent seasonal camps.

Staying in or near one place for a long time enabled craftsmen to develop tools that would have been too heavy to carry on long treks after wandering herds of wild animals. New tools included the nutting stone, with cuplike depressions that held nuts in place while they were being cracked; the milling stone for crushing seeds into a powder; soapstone cooking vessels; and various wood-working tools for building homes and making canoes. Some of these new tools were not pressure-flaked and chipped; they were pecked and pounded into a rough shape and then smoothed to a high polish with sand and other abrasives.

For hunting deer, men used a spear-thrower (atlatl) that enabled them to throw the spear with greater force by effectively lengthening the arm. To bring the spear thrower into better balance and further increase the force of the throw, hunters attached polished and sculptured weights, called atlatl weights or bannerstones. Spears were tipped with broad-bladed points that were notched at the corners so they would stay embedded in the flesh of wounded animals as they fled through the forest. Hunters followed wounded animals, sometimes for days, to kill and butcher them.

By three or four thousand years ago, Native Americans had learned to make very good use of each region's resources.

Nowhere, except at the frigid tip of South America, was life more difficult for the Native Americans than in the desert areas. Here people endured the parching heat of summer and cold winter nights. They learned to braid yucca fibers into sandals to protect their feet from sharp stones as they moved long distances in search of seeds, but there never were enough animal skins to provide warmth in winter. Hunters who preferred antelope, jack rabbits, and bighorn sheep were often thankful for lizards, rodents, locusts, and ant eggs. Teeth of the desert people were worn to the pulp from chewing grit along with cacti and other tough plants. The wads of indigestible fibers they spit out are found at many campsites. Needing light-weight containers for carrying food and water, the desert people became expert basket makers. Special baskets were used to gather, winnow, and parch seeds as small as those of wild grasses. Some baskets were tight enough to hold liquids; others were smeared with pitch and used as water jugs.

Between seven and eight thousand years ago, the desert people who lived in the Valley of Tehuacan in south-central Mexico began some experiments that would eventually benefit all mankind. These people, whose lives depended on finding small animals and collecting seeds, had to be very observant in order to survive. They noticed that seeds sprout to produce a new crop of plants. Finally someone—possibly a woman, for women did nearly all of the gathering—began planting seeds of favorite foods and giving them special care.

Because the Valley of Tehuacan was very dry, the first planter did not have to clear forests or sod. Only a stick was needed to stir the soil and make holes for the seeds. The skill lay in knowing when to plant the seeds to best take advantage of the scant rainfall and limited growing season. At any rate, the experiment was successful. Three thousand years later, about four thousand years before the present, the people in this valley were obtaining one-third of their diet from cultivated foods. The food gatherers had become food producers and exporters of farming technology. In another thousand years—three thousand years before the present—corn, squash, and gourds that originated in Mexico were being planted by Native Americans living in North Carolina.

One of the first foods to be cultivated in the Western Hemisphere was a grass that came to be known as maize, or Indian corn. Pumpkins and gourds may have been planted, though probably by accident, as early as nine thousand years ago. Other early crops in the New World included avocados, chili peppers, squash, beans, and tobacco. Once the idea of farming spread, Native Americans went on to cultivate and improve potatoes, sweet potatoes,

During the early part of the Archaic Period, Native American hunters invented the spear thrower, or atlatl, which enabled them to hurl their spears with increased power and accuracy. The atlatl consisted of a short wooden shaft with a bone or antler hook at one end. The hook fitted into the end of the spear shaft when the atlatl was held below and parallel to it. Grasping the spear thrower with one hand and hooking the index finger over the spear shaft, the hunter drew back his arm to aim the weapon. The spear shaft was released during the throw, and the atlatl, still firmly grasped by the hunter, swung away from the shaft, effectively lengthening the hunter's arm during the follow through.

manioc, peanuts, pineapples, green peppers, tomatoes, papayas, vanilla, cacao for chocolate, cotton for fiber, and more than a hundred other useful plants. From trees and shrubs they learned to extract dyes, rubber, quinine, salicylic acid for aspirin, sweet sap for making syrup and sugar, and chicle for chewing gum. If we removed from our kitchens, medicine cabinets, and stores all the products originally cultivated by the Native Americans, we would feel greatly deprived.

American Indians were the first to cultivate approximately one-half of the crops that now make up the world's total food supply. Two of these—corn and potatoes—rank with wheat and rice as the most important sources of food worldwide.

Although men often brought young wild animals home for the amusement and education of the children, Native Americans did not have many domesticated animals. There were guinea pigs, turkeys, and ducks in addition to dogs, which probably arrived with the immigrants who came across the Bering Strait at the end of the Ice Age. Dogs pulled sleds in the Arctic and the travois on the Plains, but there were no widely distributed pack animals. Buffalo (bison) were completely unwilling to work for man, but llamas and alpacas reluctantly carried small loads in the Andes. Horses and camels became extinct; cows, pigs, and a new stock of horses did not arrive in North America until there were ocean-going ships large enough to carry them. Lacking animals to pull them, Native Americans built no wagons or war chariots. Wheels were useful only in making children's toys.

Small canoes traveled the lakes and rivers of North and South America, and large canoes carried merchants in a coastal trade along the Gulf of Mexico and in the Caribbean. Trade paths went over high mountains, from the headwaters of one river to those of another, and through great forests, but the lack of an easy water route between the major cultural centers slowed the exchange of ideas. Had the New World been blessed with large, docile pack animals or a shallow inland sea, such as the Mediterranean of the Old World, the first Europeans to cross the Atlantic Ocean might have discovered a civilization as technologically advanced as their own.

American Indians did not have any large, easily domesticated animals to pull wagons or carry heavy loads. Dogs pulled the travois across the Great Plains, and high in the Andes Mountains llamas carried small loads. Canoes, however, were the most widespread form of transportation for people and goods. For this reason, Indian settlements tended to be along waterways.

Breech cloth
Chancay culture (Peru)
ca. AD 1000-1470

Doll
Chancay culture (Peru)
ca. AD 1000-1470

Shirt vicuña
Nazca culture (Peru)
ca. 100 BC-AD 600

Carrying cloth, alpaca and cotton
Nazca culture (Peru)
ca. 200 BC-AD 700

Shaped bag, alpaca and cotton
Inca culture (Peru)
ca. AD 1438-1532

Cocoa leaf carrying cloth
alpaca and cotton
Nazca culture (Peru)
ca. 200 BC-AD 700

Chuspa, alpaca and cotton
Central coast (Peru)
ca. AD 1000-1470

The most advanced cultures in the Western Hemisphere prior to the arrival of European explorers were the Inca of Peru, the Maya of southern Mexico and Central America, and the Aztec of Mexico. The early development of agriculture and methods for drainage and irrigation allowed these Indians to build cities—some with populations of nearly one hundred thousand people—and to develop great skill in pottery making, stone carving, metalworking, and weaving cloth from wool and cotton. Wherever mineral deposits were near the surface, Native Americans learned to mine and use gold, silver, and copper. They learned to heat metals to harden them without making them brittle. In time they undoubtedly would have learned to make bronze and work with iron. Like the Egyptians, some of the Incas used hollow reeds to make boats. The Maya produced plant-fiber paper for their art and books. These accordion-folded books were also made of animal skins. Maya and Aztec pyramids rival those of Egypt.

Although Native Americans lacked an alphabet, they made extensive use of pictographs, especially for keeping a record of passing time. The Maya developed a type of hieroglyphic writing somewhat like that of the Egyptians. The Aztecs had excellent calendars and a system similar to Roman numerals, but much easier to use. Incas used *quipus* for their accounting system and also as a memory aid for reciting history or poetry. The *quipu* could be worn as a pendant around the neck of the *quipu* keeper. From the circular main cord hung many smaller cords of different colors. Knots tied in a cord of one color might indicate the quantity of corn harvested in a governmental district during a certain season; cords of different colors might record other crops, livestock, or taxes to be paid. The *quipu* keeper memorized the meaning of each knot and recited the information when a government official needed a report. A runner wearing a *quipu* could carry messages swiftly from one city to another over paved roadways that extended from Ecuador down through Chile.

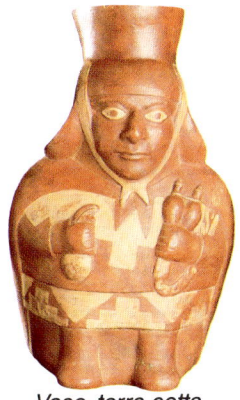

Vase, terra cotta
Moche culture (Peru)
ca. AD 200-500

Beaker, gold
Chimu culture (Peru)
ca. AD 1000-1470

Double-spout bottle
terra cotta with polychrome
Nazca culture (Peru)
ca. AD 100-300

Cylinder vase, terra cotta
Maya culture (Mexico)
classic period ca. AD 300-900

Incensario
terra cotta with polychrome
Maya culture (Mexico)
ca. AD 700-900

Ruins of the Great Temple of Tenochtitlan, liturgical center of the Aztec Empire, have been excavated in Mexico City. The shrine on the right was for the worship of Huitzilopochtli, the god of war (above right). The shrine on the left honored Tlaloc, the rain god (above center), whose consort was Chalchiuhtlicue, goddess of water from springs and seas (above left). She was also associated with earth, salt, and maize.

Inca, Aztec, and related cultures were destroyed in the sixteenth century AD by Spanish invaders, who enslaved the people and melted down their gold and silver works of art for shipment to Europe. In return for these riches, the conquistadors brought to South and Middle America devastating diseases, domesticated horses, and the Roman Catholic religion. During the past one hundred years, archaeologists have excavated the ruined Indian cities, many long covered with jungle or lying beneath buildings of Spanish architecture, and revealed how great they were.

Well before the Spanish explorers arrived, the construction of pyramidal mounds had spread to many parts of the United States. Irrigation techniques developed in Mexico made farming possible in the southwestern United States. Cultivation of cotton promoted weaving of cloth. Art flourished. Some extremely large drawings and carvings on rock surfaces are thought to have been part of an ancient system for determining the winter solstice, the shortest day of the year and an important event in some Indian cultures.

Along the Mississippi River and its tributaries, pyramidal mounds were built around plazas. Living in the southern Appalachian Mountains and in much of the land between the mountains and the great river, the Cherokees became part of this advanced Mississippian culture. Cherokees probably looked upon their neighbors in the lowlands of eastern North Carolina as being backward or old-fashioned.

Some mound builders, apparently Creek Indians from Georgia and Alabama, moved into the upper Pee Dee River valley between AD 1300 and AD 1400, displacing the Woodland people. At Town Creek Indian Mound, near Mount Gilead in Montgomery County, we can still see the newcomers' work. The palisade and other wooden structures of this ceremonial center have been rebuilt. Even the site of the post for their ball games has been found. Long-handled racquets and a hard, leather ball were used in a very rough version of field hockey. The object was to use the racquet to throw the ball so it would strike the post as high as possible. A hit above a mark about halfway up the post counted one point; striking the skull atop the post counted five points. The first side to score twenty points won the game and honors second only to those gained in battle. Called by a name that translates as "little brother of war," this game was the predecessor of lacrosse. During the 1500s, the mound builders withdrew, and descendants of the original settlers reclaimed the territory. Town Creek Indian Mound remains as mute testimony of this brief episode in the history of North Carolina.

Town Creek Indian Mound in Montgomery County, N.C., is a reconstructed Indian ceremonial center.

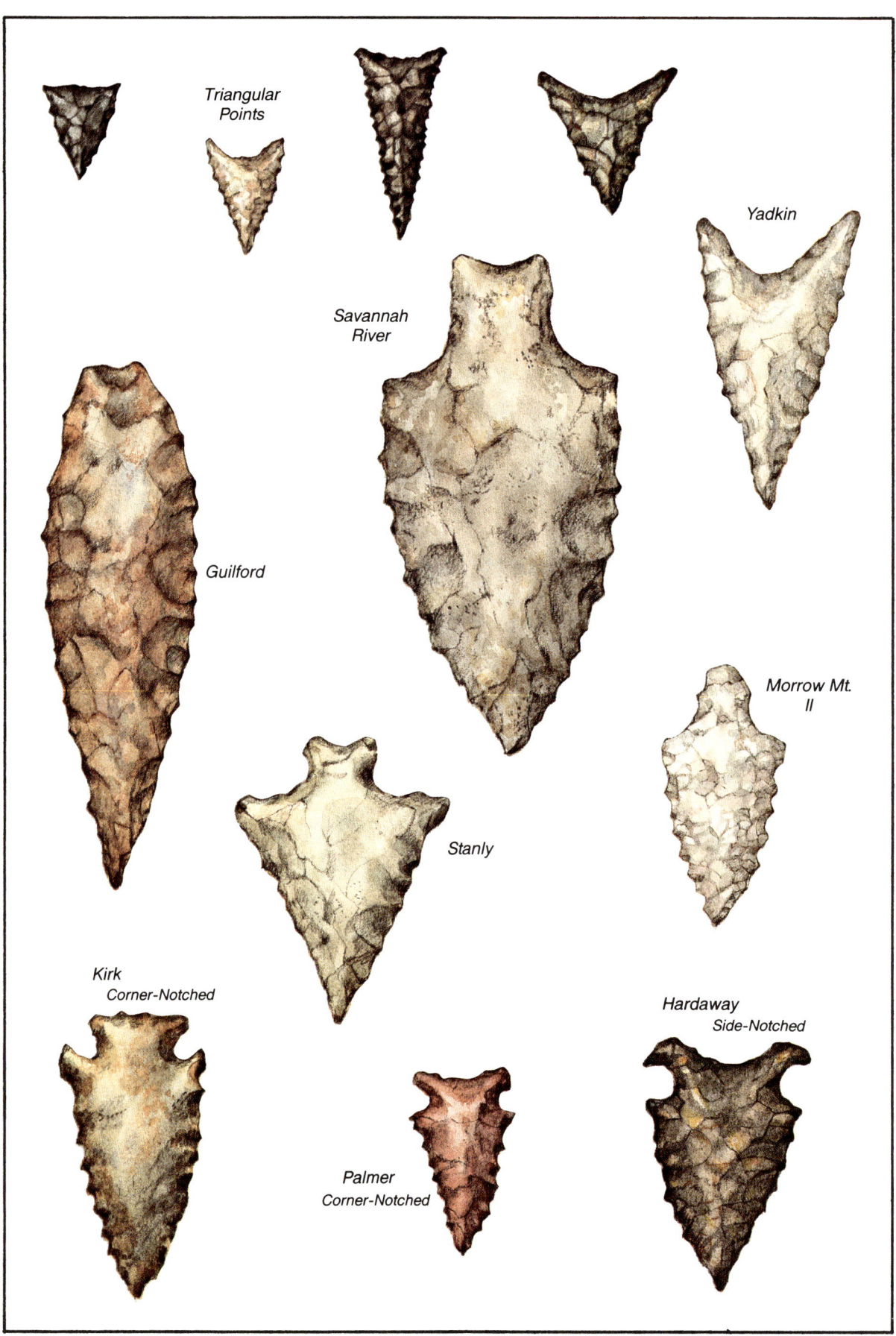

Native Americans, like people throughout the world, engaged in warfare. Those tribes with large settlements and authoritarian governments tended to be more aggressive than were the tribes that lived in small villages and made decisions with the consent of the people. Eastern Woodland Indians fought mostly to defend their tribal lands, homes, and planted crops or to avenge some wrong, usually the killing of a tribe member. Indians believed that the spirit of a murdered kinsman could not rest until those responsible had been killed. Generally, a small number of men—using stealth and the cover of night, communicating with sign language and birdcalls—raided the offending tribe and evened the score. Occasionally, enemies were ambushed by daylight.

War parties a hundred strong were very rare; pitched battles were almost unheard of. The Iroquois, however, were skilled in military tactics, assembled large war parties, and even wore wooden armor until firearms and metal arrow and spear points made such protection useless. Their guerrilla strategies for frontier fighting influenced the tactics of George Washington and his Revolutionary soldiers in their campaigns against the British troops.

Indians could be very cruel to their victims. Corpses were sometimes dismembered to provide proof of a successful raid or mutilated to deny the enemy full enjoyment of the afterlife. Scalping, which was common in Central and South America, appears to have been uncommon in North America prior to the arrival of European settlers. The most respected captives were tortured or burned alive, so they could show their bravery. Other captives were taken into the tribe as slaves or even adopted to replace family members killed in battle. Maintaining the strength of the tribe was more important than punishing the captives.

Before condemning the Indians' behavior or calling them savages, we should recall who cheered while lions devoured Christians in the Colosseum, who invented the rack and the guillotine, and who burned witches and religious dissenters at the stake. No culture has a monopoly on Man's inhumanity to Man. American Indians were, on the whole, no worse in their dealings with one another than the European people of the same time. In some respects the Indians may have been superior, particularly in their generosity toward strangers.

All projectile points pictured at left were illustrated at actual size from artifacts found in North Carolina. The approximate times that these spear and arrow points were used can be determined by consulting the endpaper chart.

The same Indian people who made war also made peace. They smoked the peace pipe (calumet), buried the hatchet (tomahawk), exchanged gifts, and made treaties. A customary peace offering was a belt of *wampumpeage* (shortened to *wampum* by the Europeans). The earliest wampum was primarily for decoration or communication and apparently consisted of wood, strings of freshwater shells, or belts interwoven with porcupine quills. Hiawatha used wampum to bring peace and unity to the Five Nations of the Iroquois and to end the blood feuds, which disrupted many tribes and were outlawed by the league. Instead of seeking revenge, the family of the bereaved was obliged to accept strings or belts of wampum from the family of the slayer. Wampum also served as credentials and symbols of authority, certified a messenger or a promise, sealed treaties, recorded laws, and eventually assumed sacred connotations. Thus the breaking of a treaty became a sacrilege. As with the *quipu* keepers of South America, specially trained and delegated people memorized and recited the messages placed on wampum. After the Iroquois began trading extensively with the tribes living in New England, the purple and white beads made from quahog shells largely replaced other materials used for wampum. Used as money by some tribes, the laboriously polished and drilled beads were made from the pearl-like inside of the shell. Each color of wampum had a special meaning. For example, white stood for women, peace, and friendship; black for men and the authority vested in them; and purple for war, death, and mourning.

Various tribes formed leagues to maintain the peace and promote trade. From 300 BC to AD 500, the Hopewell confederacy stretched from the Atlantic Ocean to Kansas. Hopewell traders brought to the Ohio River valley copper from Michigan, mica and other minerals from western North Carolina, shells from the Atlantic Ocean and the Gulf of Mexico, and obsidian (volcanic glass) from a site now within Yellowstone National Park. Prior to the arrival of European settlers, the Cherokee Nation comprised seven clans that claimed most of Kentucky and Tennessee and adjacent parts of Alabama, Georgia, South Carolina, North Carolina, Virginia, and West Virginia. The seven-sided council house of the central government could accommodate about five hundred delegates. In AD 1570 the Mohawk, Oneida, Onondaga, Cayuga, and Seneca tribes reorganized the Five Nations, or the Iroquois Longhouse, under the leadership of Hiawatha and Dekanawida. In 1722 the Tuscarora of North Carolina moved to New York, and around 1735 they joined the Iroquois Longhouse, making a confederation known as the Six Nations. Although it broke up during the Revolutionary War, when all but the Oneida and Tuscarora joined the British side, the league survives in modified form to the present time.

Wampum *Quipu Keeper*

Eighteenth-century European philosophers of the Enlightenment movement, including Rousseau and Montesquieu, were profoundly influenced by the Iroquois political and philosophical traditions. When men like Benjamin Franklin and Thomas Jefferson began looking for ways to unite the colonies to resist unfair taxation and other acts of the British Parliament, they not only read Plato, John Locke, and the French philosophers but also turned to the Iroquois and other Indian peoples for advice and encouragement.

At the Albany Conference of 1754, Old Hendrick of the Mohawks addressed the colonial delegates and urged them to overcome their disunity in relations with the Indian people by emulating the Iroquois League. The resulting Albany Plan of Union was in many respects similar to the Iroquoian plan of government, a system of balance and compromise with each tribe remaining independent though united with the others for trade, defense, and other matters that could not be handled adequately by the individual tribes. The Iroquois Confederacy functioned by the consent of the governed and recognized the need for freedom of speech and freedom of religion. Although the Albany Plan was not adopted by the colonies, it was not forgotten. When framers of the Constitution of the United States gave the federal government far more power than did the Albany Plan, Jefferson and others insisted upon adding the Bill of Rights to preserve the essential elements of political freedom and unity through discussion and consensus.

Practical-minded American colonists, mostly illiterate and unaware of Greek democracy or Enlightenment philosophy, favored adoption of the Constitution and the Bill of Rights at least in part because they had seen the principles of democracy functioning effectively among the Iroquois and other Indians who lived in the thirteen original colonies. Thus the Indian legacy of freedom, brotherhood, and unity helped to shape the political foundations of the United States.

The form of tribal government varied greatly from time to time and place to place. In some cultures, the Aztec for example, the citizens were virtually slaves of the ruler. Some tribes had two leaders, one for warfare and one for hunting and husbandry. Most of the North American tribal councils were very democratic, with decisions reached by consensus. Matters of importance were discussed in council meetings, where each person had an opportunity to speak without interruption. Although the elders were respected, their advice was not necessarily followed. Decisions were based on the welfare of the tribe rather than on a desire for personal glory or freedom.

By the time Christopher Columbus reached the New World in AD 1492, about 500 years ago, the Native Americans had settled every part of the two continents. In some places, such as the jungles of the Amazon River, there were but a few people living under extremely primitive conditions. At the southern tip of South America, food was so difficult to obtain that individual families hunted alone. Passing this bleak land by ship in 1520, Ferdinand Magellan saw huge campfires and named the place Tierra del Fuego—Land of Fire. In other places, such as in the Pacific Northwest, people carved elaborate totems and lived in plank houses fitted together with pegs. In the arid Southwest, the Pueblo Indians lived in many-storied community dwellings made of stone or adobe (sun-dried mud bricks). The Eskimos and

Aleuts perfected techniques for hunting sea mammals, including whales; life was hard, but food and skins for warm clothing were usually plentiful. Indians in the northeastern United States and adjacent Canada also hunted whales and seals, but much of their food came from the forest. The Iroquois of New York and Ontario built houses up to 100 feet long. Some longhouses sheltered eight to ten related families. In the great centers of culture, the residents of large cities and towns imported agricultural products and exported the work of skilled artisans. At least small quantities of luxury goods reached all but the most remote settlements.

Columbus was met off the coast of Honduras by a merchant canoe carrying a crew of twenty-five and a cargo of clothing and copper bells. Ancestors of those in the canoe had crossed Asia, North America, and much of Central America. Ancestors of those aboard Columbus' ship had migrated to the lands bordering the Mediterranean Sea and stayed there until, encouraged by sturdy sailing ships and instruments for navigation, they began to explore the great oceans. Columbus set out to find a shorter, easier route to the commercial riches of India, the name Europeans of his time commonly called all of Asia—China and Japan as well as India. Believing that he had reached his intended destination, he called the people he met "Indios," the Spanish word for Indians. Columbus was, in the broad sense of the word, perfectly correct. He just found the "Indios" on the wrong continent.

4

Native Americans in North Carolina

When the first Europeans sailed along the coast of North Carolina, they saw here, as elsewhere along the Atlantic seaboard, smoke from the fires of many villages. North Carolina was not a vast wilderness. It was a region settled by people who had developed a way of life adapted to surviving, and even living rather comfortably, in a woodland environment. When John White and his colonists came to Roanoke Island in 1585, Native Americans had been occupying that area for thousands of years.

The first North Carolinians were nomadic food gatherers who used bone and flaked-stone tools for hunting, fishing, dressing skins, and making clothing and ornaments. These Paleo-Indians probably lived in a cliff shelter or a simple lean-to made of long sticks propped against a tree trunk or embankment. The lean-to may have been covered with bark or skins to keep out the rain or snow. Household goods probably included bone sewing needles, a grinding stone and mortar to crush nuts and seeds, a few baskets made from bark, and bowls hollowed from pieces of wood that were naturally shaped like bowls. Cooking was done on a spit over an open fire, in hot ashes, and in skin-lined pits in the ground, where water could be heated with hot stones. The first Paleo-Indians may have reached North Carolina as early as fourteen thousand years before the present (BP). Although the remains of mastodons, bison, and other Ice Age mammals have been found in North Carolina and elsewhere in the Southeast, little, if any, direct evidence suggests that they were killed by Paleo-Indian hunters. Except in the Appalachian Mountains, the Ice Age ended early in the Southeast. Mixed deciduous and coniferous forests already covered most of the region some twelve thousand years ago, and conditions probably were no longer suitable for herds of big-game animals when the Paleo-Indians arrived. Instead, the

Continued on page 43

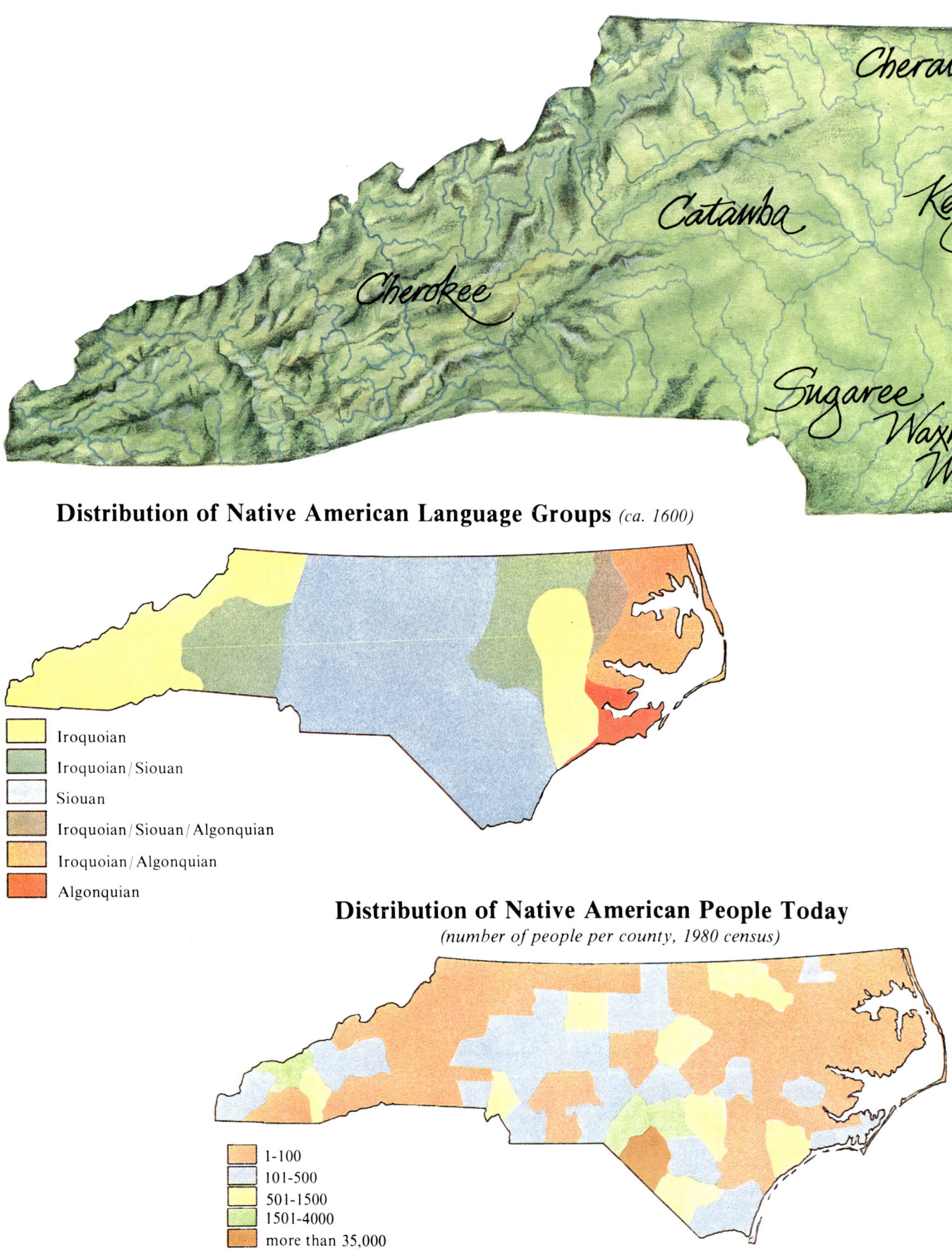

Distribution of Native American Language Groups (ca. 1600)

- Iroquoian
- Iroquoian/Siouan
- Siouan
- Iroquoian/Siouan/Algonquian
- Iroquoian/Algonquian
- Algonquian

Distribution of Native American People Today
(number of people per county, 1980 census)

- 1-100
- 101-500
- 501-1500
- 1501-4000
- more than 35,000

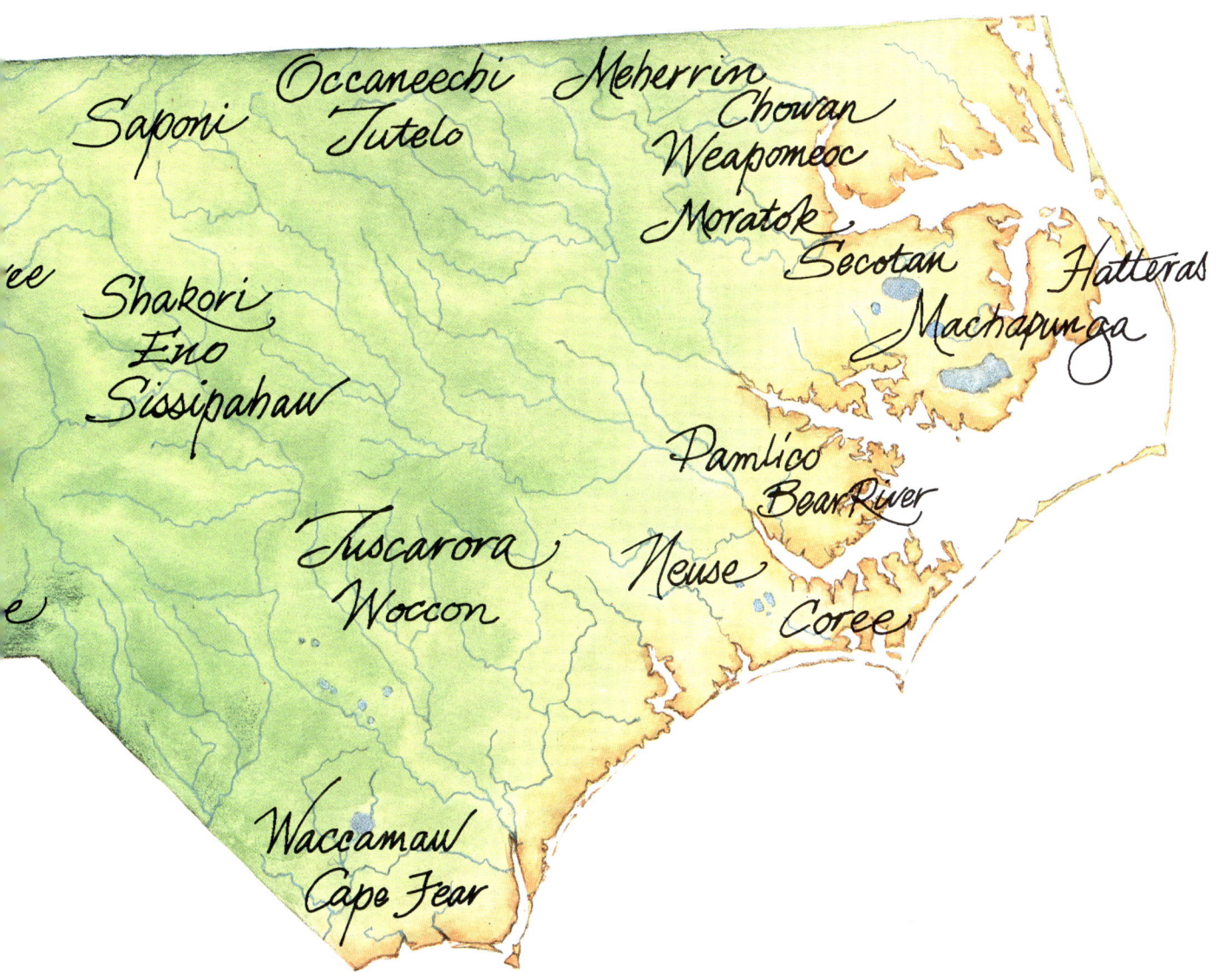

North Carolina in 1585

Native Americans were living in all parts of North Carolina when the first European settlers arrived in 1585. Many of the names that appeared on John White's map of the northeastern part of the state are still in use, though perhaps with a modified spelling. On present-day maps, many other Indian words designate counties, cities, and physiographic features throughout the state and nation.

Using a hard stone lashed with sinew to a wooden handle, the carver chips a piece of soapstone to form the underside of a cooking vessel. Once the shape is right, the bowl will be polished with sand or some other abrasive. Soapstone, also known as steatite, has a soapy or oily feeling. Composed mostly of talc, it varies in color from white through gray to green and usually contains small amounts of other minerals. Although soapstone is more easily worked than most rocks, it tolerates high temperatures and is not affected by acids.

first Carolinians seem to have relied on hunting the white-tail deer and other modern species of mammals.

From about ten thousand BP until nearly three thousand BP, the Archaic Period, the Native Americans in North Carolina hunted deer, bear, and elk with the spear thrower and used flaked-stone tools. They lived in temporary huts—probably round, wooden frames covered with bark or skins. Women used crude baskets and soapstone cooking vessels. Archaic people also made polished-stone axe heads grooved for fitting to a handle. Much of the stone used for the flaked tools came from Morrow Mountain in Stanly County. This site is now a state park, and visitors can see the many pieces of flaked stone left behind by the craftsmen.

The earliest signs of horticulture in North Carolina date from the Early Woodland Period (1000 BC to 300 BC), when climate and vegetation were about the same as they are today except for the extensive virgin forests that were later cleared by European settlers. In this state the Early Woodland Period was really just a continuation of the Archaic Period. The Indian people began to build permanent homes in settlements beside streams. Here the soil was enriched by floods, and waterways provided convenient routes for trade. In the center of the house was a rock-lined fire pit for cooking meals and warming the house. Basket making improved, polished-stone tools became common, pottery making developed, and hunters began using the bow and arrow.

The origin of the bow and arrow is unknown. Some of the earliest evidence of hunting with the bow and arrow came from the far north, where Eskimo-like immigrants from Asia lived among the Eskimos about four to five thousand years ago. These people disappeared, but their small stone tools, called microliths, preserve their craftsmanship. By 2,500 years ago, bows and arrows were used all over North and South America. It is likely that this effective weapon was invented at several different places in both the Old World and the New.

The Middle Woodland Period (300 BC to AD 800) in North Carolina corresponds with the Hopewell Period of the Middle Atlantic States and Ohio River valley.

The Late Woodland Period, which began about AD 800 and lasted until the 1600s, was marked by the building of earthen pyramidal mounds. Although they did not construct these mounds, the Algonquians had a well-developed Late Woodland society when the first European settlers arrived in North Carolina in the 1580s. Throughout North Carolina, Indian people were still dependent on hunting and gathering food, but agriculture was important for maintaining the sizable settlements. Villages had several different kinds of structures, including impressive council lodges. In the coastal plain, rectangular longhouses were more numerous than huts with conical roofs. In the piedmont and mountains, round structures outnumbered the rectangular ones. During the Late Woodland Period, pottery improved in quality and was beautifully decorated with complicated designs. Copper and polished-stone celts, tools shaped like chisels or hand axes, occurred but were not common.

Twenty-eight tribes are known to have lived in North Carolina at the time of European contact. Based on language, these people can be grouped into three families: Iroquoian, Siouan, and Algonquian. The Iroquoian tribes included the mountain-dwelling Cherokee, who spoke at least three different dialects, and the Tuscarora, Meherrin, and Coree of the central coastal plain. The fifteen Siouan tribes were mostly in the piedmont and southern coastal plain: the Cape Fear, Catawba, Cheraw, Eno, Keyauwee, Occaneechi, Saponi, Shakori, Sissipahaw, Sugaree, Tutelo, Waccamaw, Wateree, Waxhaw, and Woccon. The Algonquian people, who migrated from the northeastern United States and eastern Canada, occupied the North Carolina coast and tidewater areas south to southern Onslow County. In eastern Virginia lived the closely related Algonquians who were dominated by the great Chief Powhatan when English settlers arrived at Jamestown in 1607. To communicate with each other, people who spoke different tongues used sign language and a simplified spoken language such as Mobilian, which was a collection of words used primarily to conduct trade in some parts of the Southeast.

North Carolina Native Americans differed as much in physical appearance as they did in language. The Algonquian speakers along the coast were of medium stature with long heads and rugged facial features. The Siouan speakers of the piedmont were small of stature with rounded heads and small, graceful facial features. The Iroquoian-speaking Cherokees were of medium stature with a rugged body build. They had round heads and faces with large, rugged features.

The North Carolina Algonquians greeted John White and helped the Roanoke colonists learn the ways of a land that was new to them. John White visited Indian villages occasionally from 1585 to 1587 and recorded what he learned in detailed drawings, maps, and a written account. Arthur Barlowe, Thomas Harriot, and Ralph Lane also recorded their experiences with the Indians. Through the efforts of these men, we know more about the customs of the Algonquians than any other tribal group living in North Carolina at that time. Because all of these tribes had some contact with each other, we believe that only minor differences existed among them.

5

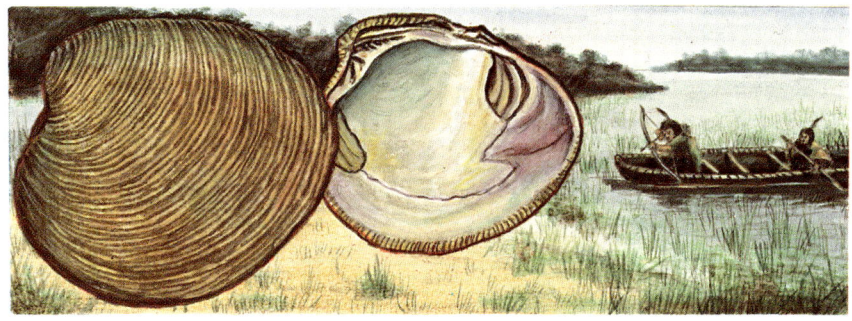

The Algonquians

Traveling by canoe, the North Carolina Algonquians (also spelled *Algonkians*) hunted, fished, and gathered shellfish in the lands bordering Albemarle and Pamlico Sounds. The total population of their twenty-five to thirty villages may have been seven to eight thousand inhabitants. Their word *poquosin*, now spelled *pocosin* and translated as "swamp on a hill" or "shallow place," is still used to designate the wet, impenetrable thickets of the Southeastern coastal plain.

Although the Algonquians lived in villages, some of them rather large, and grew a number of different crops, the people were dependent on hunting and fishing for most of their meat. Village life was organized around the seasonal hunts and the farming chores. If the soil became infertile or firewood became scarce, the whole village probably moved to a different site. Several moves might bring them back to a place formerly occupied.

Most of the settlements were along waterways, and where water was not naturally present, the Indians dug ponds. At least two town plans were followed. In some villages the buildings were clustered around a central plaza. Settlements like that often were surrounded by a palisade, a tall fence made of poles stuck in the ground close to one another. Where the ends of the two semicircular fences overlapped, the two rows were set wide enough apart to permit residents to come and go. The height of the poles and narrowness of the passageway discouraged entry of wild animals and provided some protection from raids by enemy tribes. The other plan was to have the huts placed along a riverbank, perhaps with a well-made street running the length of the settlement.

45

The towne of Pomeiock and true forme of their howses, couered and enclosed some wth matts, and some wth barcks of trees. All compassed abowt wth smale poles stock thick together in stedd of a wall.

In either case, the village had a council house that was built like the dwellings, but much larger. There also may have been a temple and a building for preparation of dead chiefs and other leaders for burial in special pits called ossuaries. Commoners apparently were buried in shallow graves, as were the dogs people had as pets.

The typical Algonquian building had a frame of upright wooden poles made from saplings, which were bent over and tied together to form an arched roof. Horizontal poles reinforced the structure. Stone axes were used

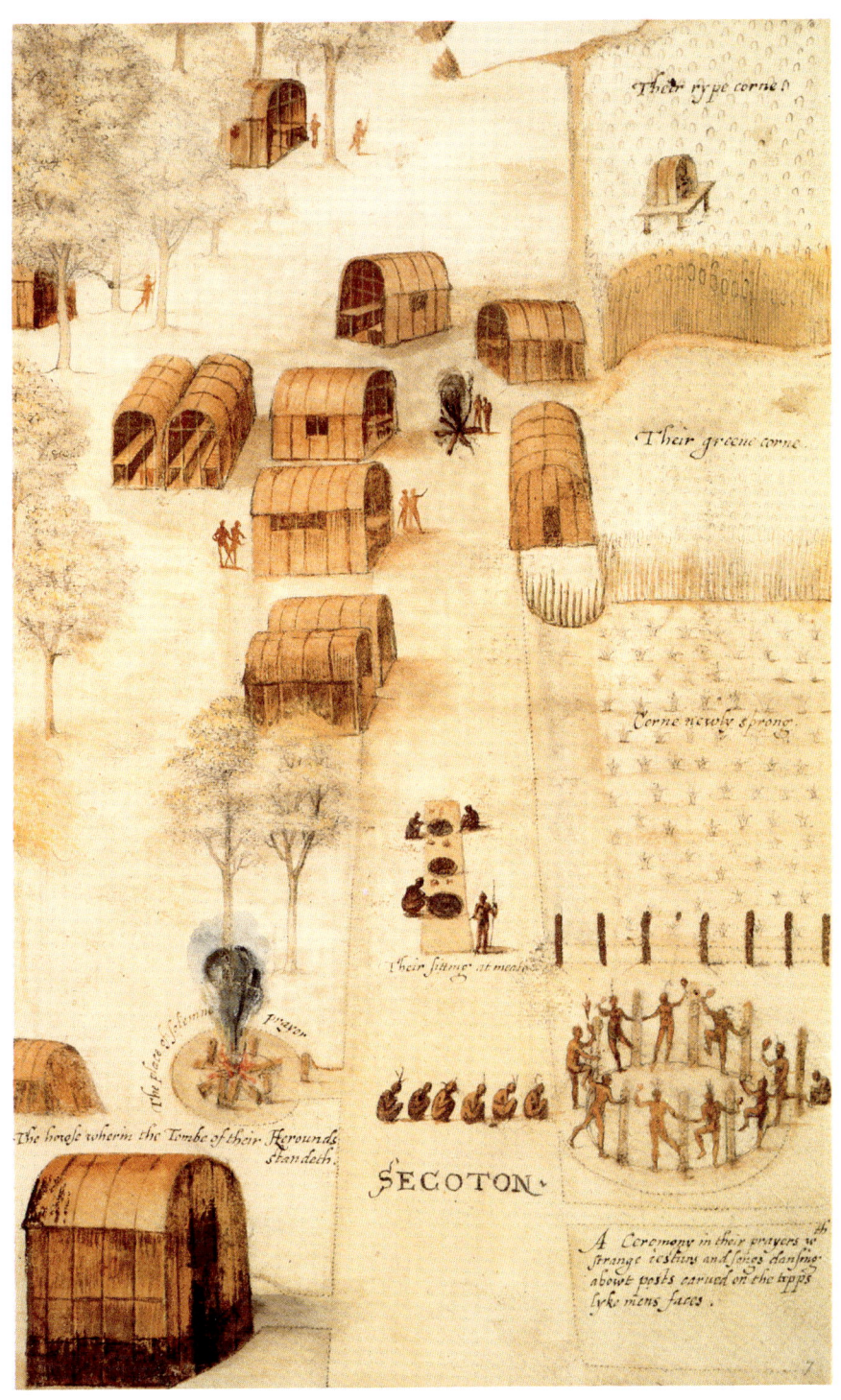

John White's drawings depict two basic village plans used by Algonquian Indians in the 1580s. On the facing page is the palisaded village of Pomeiooc, and above is a village without an enclosure. Beside the farming village are three fields of corn, indicating three different plantings in a single season. In the foreground villagers are participating in the Green Corn Ceremony, which took place when the new crop of corn was first ready for harvest.

for chopping wood to make houses. The frame was covered with sheets of bark or with woven rush mats that could be turned up as necessary for light and ventilation. The length of a house, 36 to 72 feet according to Thomas Harriot, was usually double the width. Each dwelling had two entrances, with a path leading to the front door. Several related family groups might live in a single longhouse, some of which were partitioned into as many as five rooms. Some longhouses even had closets and, above the front door, symbols identifying the occupants. Furniture consisted of long tables or benches, which may have been used for sleeping as well as for sitting and dining.

The various Algonquian tribes were small monarchies. Each ruler wore a copper badge of authority and had his own symbol, which was tattooed on the people to show their tribal affiliation. Each tribe had definite political boundaries and a formalized religion, though shaman practitioners perpetuated the customs of the ancient hunting-society religion. Below the ruling class came the nobility and the commoners. The rulers, nobility, and priests lived in the towns, but most of the commoners probably lived in the countryside.

Because all descent, including the succession of rulers, was matrilineal, women had a good bit of influence in the home and in tribal affairs. A child's relatives were his mother and her brothers, sisters, and mother in addition to his own brothers and sisters. The mother's brother usually represented the family in public affairs. If a woman of one class married a man of another, their children were of her class, not his. Among the New England Algonquians, the widow of a deceased sachem (chief) might succeed him.

Marriage was primarily an economic and social arrangement, lacking the legal and religious significance associated with this custom in European cultures. With the consent of the first wife, a man could take a second wife, and divorce was mostly by mutual consent. The informality of marriage customs does not mean there was no romance among Indian people. Young men made courting flutes from reeds or the wood of willow trees and composed special songs they played at night outside the home of the maiden of their choice. These flutes may have been simple or elaborately carved, but they always were decorated with feathers and the figure of a bird.

Customs discouraged the accumulation of many possessions, and people who did so were regarded with suspicion and disapproval. Clothing, ornaments, skin marked by patterns of tattoos or scars, and the use of body paint indicated a person's tribe and rank.

Before colonial times, almost all clothing was made of buckskin, with the edges slit to form tassels. Such clothes were much too hot for summertime comfort in most parts of the Southeast. In warm weather children went naked, and men and women customarily wore only a breech clout, a long piece of material suspended from a belt and hanging down in the front and back, or perhaps only in the front. Such scant clothing shocked the English, but Native Americans did not consider the human body a source of embarrassment. Modesty was shown by the way people acted, not by what they wore. In cold weather Indians wore heavy clothing, often including animal skins with the fur turned toward the wearer's body.

On special occasions, such as going on a hunt, a man might hang a long animal tail from the back of his belt. Buckskin and snakeskin were often used for belts. A buckskin belt might be decorated with designs made from porcupine quills. Although Woodland Indians did not have looms for weaving cloth, they were skillful at finger-weaving pliable fibers into belts.

Tanning a deer hide into buckskin for use in clothing was a laborious process. First, the hide was removed from the animal. Next the excess flesh had to be scraped from the skin without cutting holes in it. Neatly folded and tied like a package, the skin was soaked in water for two to four days, depending on the size of the animal. Upon removal from the water, the hide was inspected for holes, and any remaining excess flesh was removed. Then the hide was laid, hair side up and hair direction toward the ground, across a debarked log that had been set in the ground in an inclined position. Here the hair was pulled from the hide with a special scraper that was pushed away from the worker. Great care was required to avoid cutting the damp hide. The hairless hide was then worked for about an hour with deer brains. Stored in dry cakes near the fireplace, brains were mixed with water, or water and ashes, before being applied to the hide. When this process was finished, the hide was stretched on a frame in direct sunlight. Now the paddle tool was used to soften the hide and remove the unwanted outer layers, one on the hair side and one on the flesh side. The hide was worked and reworked until the outer hides began to come off in small rolls. The final step—and one not used by the Plains Indians—was to smoke the hides to produce a golden brown color and to keep them from becoming stiff when wet. The hide was rolled into a cylinder and hung from a frame built over a pit in the ground. Smoke and heat from the fire in the pit went upward through the hide "chimney." When one side was thoroughly smoked, the hide was rolled the other way, and the same process was followed. Once the smoking was completed, the buckskin was ready for the seamstress.

Buckskin was used for drumheads, pouches, belts, aprons (breech clouts), capes, shirts, wrap-around skirts, moccasins, and leggings. Bone awls and needles were used to sew the pieces together with sinews. The tubular leggings, which provided warmth and protected men's legs from brush and thorns, and the breech clout were suspended from a single belt. A cape or shirt and moccasins completed the man's winter garb. Dressed in a cape, knee-length wrap-around skirt, knee-high wrap-around leggings tied in place

Tanning a deer hide into buckskin was a laborious process. Once the hide was taken from the animal, the excess flesh had to be removed. This woman is using a stone scraper to clean the hide. She is working very carefully to avoid making holes in the skin. Later the hide will be treated to remove the hair and the inner and outer layers of skin. The finished buckskin will be used to make clothing, moccasins, pouches, or perhaps a drumhead.

with sashes, and moccasins, Indian women should have appeared modest enough to suit the most particular Englishman.

Both men and women wore bone, copper, shell, and polished-stone beads as well as animal claws and teeth. Men often outdid the women in their ornamentation by wearing earrings, bracelets, copper breastplates, or strings of pearls. Copper bells were worn by dancers. Sometimes the men wore long capes made of fur or feathers. Fans were made from the wings of large birds, such as the turkey.

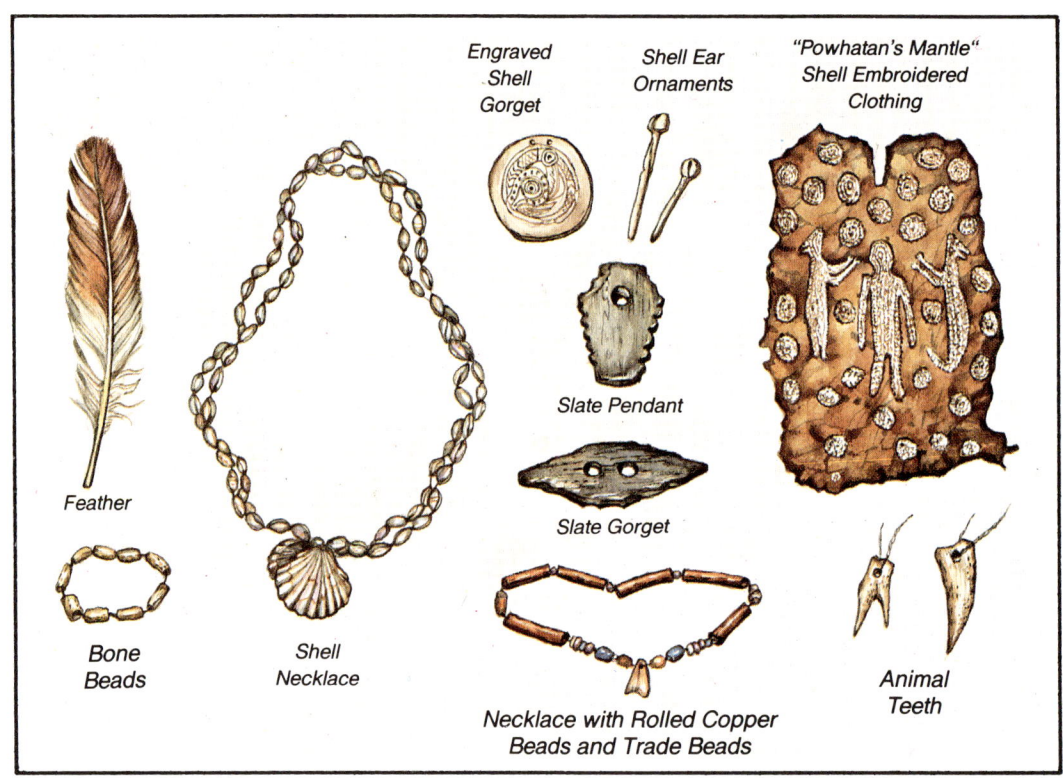

Algonquian men often stuck feathers in their hair. In some tribes, such as the Cherokee, one or two feathers might be held in place by a headband. Animal tails were also used as head ornaments. Among the Plains Indians, these simple decorations evolved into elaborate headdresses made of materials that included feathers, fur, and porcupine quills. The style chosen by dashing young warriors was the roach, so named by the English because it looks like the clipped mane of a horse. The full war bonnet, considered becoming only to men with wrinkled faces, never was as common as the cowboy and Indian shows have led us to believe.

Some men wore their hair closely cropped or plucked on the sides and fairly long on top, like a cockscomb—a style popularly called the Mohawk. Others allowed the hair to grow long, hanging down in the back or tied in a loose knot. The English thought that Indian men had no beards; actually, they plucked their scant facial hair with clamshell tweezers.

The women often wore their hair with bangs across the forehead, short hair covering the ears, and long hair in back either hanging loose or tied into a bun. Some used bone hairpins. In another style, favored by both men and women, the hair was parted in the middle and braided on both sides. Beaded braid wraps or hair ties and other accessories were usually identified with a particular tribe.

Algonquian priests wore a distinctive hair style and a short cloak of hare skin quilted with the fur outward. Native Americans believed in a great creator as well as in the many helper dieties that he made. They believed in the immortality of the human soul and in a form of heaven. All things were symbolically related, and natural forces were described in kinship terms.

The moon was a grandmother who helped people in the dark and measured time. The sun was an elder brother who provided warmth and daylight. Various plants and animals were sisters and brothers. Therefore, the hunter who killed an animal asked the forgiveness of its spirit so that game would continue to be plentiful on the hunting grounds.

The construction of a new weir for catching fish, the harvest of the first corn of the season, or any other special event was an occasion for ceremony. Indians took special care in growing and curing a plant called *uppowoc*, which they smoked in clay pipes. The elbow-shaped pipe was often decorated with figures of animals, and the short stem was lengthened by inserting a hollow reed. Smoking *uppowoc* seems to have been an important part of Indian life, especially during ceremonial or festive occasions. Powder made from this plant was sprinkled on fires or waters during ceremonies. Today we know this plant as tobacco. However, the tobacco grown by Native Americans contained a much higher proportion of nicotine than the leaf used in present-day smoking products.

The shaman, or medicine man, wore a small black bird fastened over one ear as a badge of office. The bag hanging from his belt held cures and sacred objects. Although he worked like other men, Indian people believed that he had special powers to drive out the evil spirits that caused illness and misfortune. He helped people become spiritually pure prior to the important events in their lives.

The Green Corn Ceremony, one of several different thanksgiving festivals, was a major event in the religious life of many native Carolinians. This ceremony marked the time in late summer when the new crop of corn could be eaten. People cleaned the council lodge and their own homes. After fasting, they bathed, extinguished old fires and started new ones, burned any food left over from the previous year, and smashed old pots, which were replaced with new ones. They also forgave all wrong-doing except murder.

The shaman, or medicine man, fastened a small black bird above one ear as a badge of office and carried a bag of cures and sacred objects attached to the belt around his waist. The shaman hunted and worked like other men, but he had special powers to drive out the evil spirits that caused illness and misfortune. Indians believed that they must be spiritually pure for major undertakings such as the first harvest of corn, the beginning of the winter hunt, and going to war. Sweathouses, earthen structures with no windows, usually were built beside streams. Hot rocks were rolled into the ovenlike buildings. Pouring water on hot rocks filled the room with steam. As the sweaty occupant emerged, he plunged into the cold water. Other means of purification included fasting, drinking emetic teas, and bathing. Physical cleanliness was a major part of spiritual cleanliness.

In the southeastern United States, Indians held in great esteem the "black drink" or "cassena," brewed from the caffeine-containing leaves of the yaupon, a holly that grows in abundance on the North Carolina coast. This tea reputedly restored lost appetites, confirmed one's health, and bestowed courage and agility in war.

Algonquian hunters used the bow and arrow for taking deer, bear, and other large game. Their characteristic triangular arrow points were made of jasper, chert, and argillite. Hunters often hid in trees or tall grass while waiting for the approach of their quarry. Another strategy for hunting deer was to don a deer skin that still had the head attached and, bending over and moving like a deer, join the herd to get a close shot. Some men were so good at imitating deer that they were accidentally shot by other hunters. Sometimes fire was used to drive game into the open. To make their hunting grounds attractive to the white-tail deer, Indians used controlled burning to clear underbrush from the forests and to maintain the meadows and the tender new growth that deer like to graze.

Algonquians also took birds, squirrels, rabbits, and other small game. Arrows used for these animals were usually sharpened reeds hardened in the fire. Snares and throwing sticks were also used but, unlike the Cherokees, the Algonquians did not use blowguns. Turkeys were hunted, often with the aid of a captive bird used as a decoy. Ducks and geese were taken at night from a canoe with a fire built on a bed of clay. The fire, which did not frighten the waterfowl, hid the hunter standing behind it. Torches were used by the Native Americans who hunted the enormous flocks of the now-extinct Passenger Pigeon. Going into the pigeon roosts, the men could kill large numbers by hitting them with sticks. Native Americans ate the flesh and melted down the fat into cooking oil.

Some descriptions of Indian villages mention large stores of bear grease and pigeon oil, both of which were used as grooming aids. Sunburn and dry skin were problems for Native Americans because they spent most of their daylight hours out-of-doors. Grease softened the skin and discouraged biting insects. Oil also was used as a hair dressing.

Men, women, and children fished, though for the men this activity did not have the great religious significance of hunting game. They used nets, traps, and bone hooks to catch fish. Algonquians built weirs, which looked much like fences, across streams or channels. Reaching the barrier of reeds woven or tied together and anchored to the bottom with poles, the fish eventually swam into a trap where they could be speared or caught in dip nets. Sometimes Indians used a plant poison to stun the fish without making their flesh unsafe to eat. In the mountains, Indians built durable, V-shaped weirs of rocks, which occasionally trap unsuspecting present-day canoeists.

Spears and most arrows were tipped with flaked-stone points. This craftsman is sitting crosslegged beside a tree stump. He is using a piece of deer antler to shape an arrowhead.

Another method of fishing practiced by the Algonquians was to go out in their canoes at night with a fire burning on a bed of clay in the bottom of the boat, as when hunting waterfowl. Attracted to the light, the fish were easy to net or spear. The many-barbed fishing spears apparently were tipped with spines of the horseshoe crab.

Constructing a dugout canoe without using iron or steel tools was a major undertaking. First a tree large enough to make the boat had to be felled, usually with the aid of small fires built at the base of the trunk. Poplar and cypress trees were commonly used because of their straightness, but

Dugout canoes were used on the rivers, lakes, and sounds of North Carolina. Some made by the coastal Algonquians were about two feet wide and more than thirty feet long. A log was gradually burned, chipped, and scraped to smooth the outside and hollow the inside. Here the craftsman is using an adz made by fastening a sharpened stone to wooden handle. Notches along the open edges of the canoe aided in burning the sides down to the desired height. In the background a small fire begins the process of felling a tree to make another canoe.

58

white cedar may have been used by the Algonquians because of its ease in working and resistance to rot. Once the limbs and bark were removed, the log was raised on supports and gradually burned, chipped, and scraped to smooth the outside and to hollow the inside. Gum and rosin were spread on the parts to be burned. Edges that should not be burned were kept wet with water. A quahog shell or an adz with a stone blade was used to gouge out the charred wood. The finished dugout canoe was one and a half to two feet wide and up to thirty-two feet long. In northern regions where suitable birch bark was available, this lighter material was preferred. Sometimes canoe frames were covered with animal skins. Indians used long poles to move their canoes over shallow water, but elsewhere they used paddles or oars.

Shellfish were held in low esteem by the Woodland Indians, but the huge mounds of shells along the coast and beside inland streams attest to the importance of this type of food. Children often brought home turtles for the stew pot and helped the women gather fruits, berries, and nuts. Native Americans made wine from grapes, but they had no corks or bottles for storing it. They also brewed beer from persimmons, honey locust pods, and other fruits and grains. Most of the year they drank water boiled with ginger, black cinnamon, or sassafras roots.

The Algonquians were farmers as well as hunters and gatherers. They usually located their garden plots along rivers where flood waters periodically

renewed the fertility of the land. Slash-and-burn methods were used to remove woodlands or grasslands prior to the first planting. Working in established fields, men used long-handled wooden hoes or mattocks to break up the land. Sitting on the ground, women worked with short peckers or parers. After the upturned stubble and weeds of the previous season had dried for a few days, the Indians burned the field. A wooden pecker (dibble) was used to make holes for the seeds, which were spaced well apart and carefully covered with dirt.

Algonquians planted corn, squash, several kinds of beans (not a major crop until AD 1000), pumpkins, sunflowers, sweet potatoes, tobacco, and gourds. The men took turns guarding the fields and scaring away birds and wild animals that might destroy the crops. These human scarecrows sat upon a platform above the growing plants. This duty was not to be taken lightly, for bears and raccoons have a great fondness for corn.

The Purple Martin is one bird Indians considered beneficial. They often cut off the limbs of young trees near their homes and hung hollowed-out gourds from the stubs. When a suitable sapling was not available, they set up poles with cross-arms to hold the gourds. Later this practice was adopted by Negro slaves, who thought martins kept hawks away from their poultry. Today many people erect elaborate martin houses because the birds help control flying insect pests.

Having smoke holes but no flues or chimneys in their houses, the Algonquians probably did most of their cooking outside over open fires. Earthen pots with rounded or conical bottoms rested on small mounds of soil and were surrounded by fire. In this manner the women boiled or stewed meat, fish, fruits, nuts, and vegetables. Wild onions and various herbs were used for seasoning, and cornmeal was used to thicken stews. Sometimes food was broiled over an open fire, with the meat or fish placed on a grill made of reeds and supported by four large stakes driven into the ground. Corn, still in the husk, was roasted in the hot ashes.

Bread was generally made from corn. Women soaked the hard kernels in lye (made by dripping water through wood ashes) to remove the husks and cause the grain to swell. Afterwards, they pounded the skinned grain (hominy) into meal. The coarse bits of hominy sifted from the meal are called grits. For variety, boiled and mashed beans, acorns, walnuts, or chestnuts were added to the cornmeal used for bread making. A substitute for butter

Indian women soaked dried corn in wood ashes lye to remove the hard skins and make the grain swell. They ground or pounded the skinned corn into meal. The woman on the left has placed corn in a hollowed-out tree stump and is using a beater to make cornmeal. The girl on the right is using a milling stone to crush seeds. In the background are longhouses typical of those made by North Carolina Algonquians.

was made from the fat of bears or Passenger Pigeons. Until honey bees, sugar cane, and sugar beets were brought to the Americas by European settlers, Indians sweetened their food with syrup and sugar obtained by boiling the sap of certain trees, especially the sugar maple and the sweet birch.

Although the Algonquians had no potter's wheel, they did make beautiful and serviceable clay containers. They mixed sand or crushed oyster, mussel, or scallop shells with clay to prevent the pot from cracking when it was heated. The base of the pot was formed with the fingers into a shallow bowl. Then clay was rolled between the palms of the hands to make long ropes. These were coiled upon the base until the pot reached the desired size and shape. The hands and clay had to be kept moist so that each additional coil could be pressed and smoothed into the one below. The completed vessel was smoothed inside and out with a river stone and decorated. Patterns were applied in several different ways. Most commonly, a wicker-type fabric was pressed against the surface so the impressions overlapped to create a textured pattern all over. Sometimes a paddle was carved with grooves or covered with a woven mat. A sharp object was used to add a pattern of lines and dots, often in the form of chevrons, triangles, or cross-hatches. To insure durability and permanent hardness, air-dried pottery was heated in the fire. After firing, the pot could be waterproofed by burning pitch inside it.

In addition to pottery, Algonquian cooks used wooden platters, bowls, spoons, and ladles. Gourds held liquids. At mealtime, Indian men and women sat facing each other on large mats made of reeds. They used their fingers to pick food from the wooden bowls and platters placed between them. One of the Roanoke colonists described the Indians as "very sober in their eating, and drinking, and consequently very long lived because they do not oppress nature."

Indian women were regarded as having great spiritual strength because they gave birth to the next generation. The newborn child was bound to a cradle board to keep his back straight. The cradle board also flattened the back of the head. Sometimes the infant's forehead was bound to shape it, without harming the brain, into the form most admired by people in his tribe. The cradle board, which had a hole that permitted removal of body

Without benefit of a potter's wheel, North Carolina Indians made beautiful and serviceable containers from coils of clay mixed with sand or crushed shells to prevent the pot from cracking when it was heated. This woman began the vessel by shaping a shallow bowl, or base, with her fingers. Now she is winding a clay coil upon the base. She is keeping her hands and the clay moist as she presses and smooths each additional coil into the one below. She will use a river stone to smooth the vessel inside and out before applying a decorative pattern. North Carolina Indians fired their pottery to make it durable but did not glaze it.

was made from the fat of bears or Passenger Pigeons. Until honey bees, sugar cane, and sugar beets were brought to the Americas by European settlers, Indians sweetened their food with syrup and sugar obtained by boiling the sap of certain trees, especially the sugar maple and the sweet birch.

Although the Algonquians had no potter's wheel, they did make beautiful and serviceable clay containers. They mixed sand or crushed oyster, mussel, or scallop shells with clay to prevent the pot from cracking when it was heated. The base of the pot was formed with the fingers into a shallow bowl. Then clay was rolled between the palms of the hands to make long ropes. These were coiled upon the base until the pot reached the desired size and shape. The hands and clay had to be kept moist so that each additional coil could be pressed and smoothed into the one below. The completed vessel was smoothed inside and out with a river stone and decorated. Patterns were applied in several different ways. Most commonly, a wicker-type fabric was pressed against the surface so the impressions overlapped to create a textured pattern all over. Sometimes a paddle was carved with grooves or covered with a woven mat. A sharp object was used to add a pattern of lines and dots, often in the form of chevrons, triangles, or cross-hatches. To insure durability and permanent hardness, air-dried pottery was heated in the fire. After firing, the pot could be waterproofed by burning pitch inside it.

In addition to pottery, Algonquian cooks used wooden platters, bowls, spoons, and ladles. Gourds held liquids. At mealtime, Indian men and women sat facing each other on large mats made of reeds. They used their fingers to pick food from the wooden bowls and platters placed between them. One of the Roanoke colonists described the Indians as "very sober in their eating, and drinking, and consequently very long lived because they do not oppress nature."

Indian women were regarded as having great spiritual strength because they gave birth to the next generation. The newborn child was bound to a cradle board to keep his back straight. The cradle board also flattened the back of the head. Sometimes the infant's forehead was bound to shape it, without harming the brain, into the form most admired by people in his tribe. The cradle board, which had a hole that permitted removal of body

Without benefit of a potter's wheel, North Carolina Indians made beautiful and serviceable containers from coils of clay mixed with sand or crushed shells to prevent the pot from cracking when it was heated. This woman began the vessel by shaping a shallow bowl, or base, with her fingers. Now she is winding a clay coil upon the base. She is keeping her hands and the clay moist as she presses and smooths each additional coil into the one below. She will use a river stone to smooth the vessel inside and out before applying a decorative pattern. North Carolina Indians fired their pottery to make it durable but did not glaze it.

Upon reaching an age of about twelve years, an Indian youth underwent special ceremonies and assumed adult responsibilities. After killing his first deer or other large animal, the young hunter gave all the meat to his elderly relatives. This act of generosity showed that he was now old enough for marriage. The adult male white-tail deer this hunter is about to shoot will provide a large hide for making buckskin and bone and antlers for making tools as well as meat for the family.

wastes, provided a safe place for the baby while the mother went about her chores. Children were treated very tenderly, but they were expected to learn at an early age to help with the gathering of food and firewood. Though rarely spanked or scolded, they were told many legends about the consequences of bad behavior.

Although Native Americans did not have a written literature, they had an extensive oral tradition that was passed on from generation to generation. In recalling an Indian feast, John Lawson said that women wearing bells at their necks and ankles danced for six hours to the music of a drum and a gourd rattle while the musicians recounted the history of the tribe. This history may have started with the creation of the Earth.

According to one myth common to East Asia and America, birds were present at the creation. Taking turns, each bird dived to the bottom of the all-encompassing waters and tried to bring up the mud that would become the land. It was the loon that succeeded. In other legends, the creator had so much work to do that he entrusted many small details to helpers who, unfortunately, were less than perfect. Chief among these was the Trickster, who in America is represented as Raven, Mink, Rabbit, or Coyote. Instructed to make rivers on which man could float from place to place and rest his weary back, the Trickster carelessly let them all flow downstream. Man has been complaining ever since. The Trickster brought man light and fire and scattered salmon roe in the stream, but he was so fond of ceremonies that he brought death to the world. Once he even pretended to be dead so he could gobble up all the grave offerings. The Trickster may have been impulsive, thoughtless, greedy, or crafty; but often his tricks misfired and made a fool of him. In one story used as a warning to children, the Trickster believed himself to be as clever as the beaver; but after diving under the ice for fish, he could not get out. Another time he tried to capture a flock of swimming ducks by tying their legs together; they took flight, carrying him along with them. And once he dived after berries he saw reflected in the water and hit his head on a stone.

Native Americans had, and still have, a poetic and sometimes humorous way of expressing themselves. Their language reflects a genuine understanding of the world around them and a deep reverence for peace, for all forms of life, and for all things beautiful.

6

The Two Roads

In the Foreword to *The Indians' Book*, a collection of songs and legends of the American Indians edited by Natalie Curtis and published in 1907, Hiamovi, chief among the Cheyennes and the Dakotas, looked back upon the history of his people and wrote:

Long ago the Great Mystery caused this land to be, and made the Indians to live in this land. Well has the Indian fulfilled all the intent of the Great Mystery for him. Through this book may men know that the Indian people was made by the Great Mystery for a purpose.

Once, only Indians lived in this land. Then came strangers from across the Great Water. No land had they; we gave them of our land. No food had they; we gave them of our corn. The strangers are become many and they fill all the country. They dig gold—from my mountains; they build houses—of the trees of my forests; they rear cities—of my stones and rocks; they make fine garments—from the hides and wool of animals that eat my grass. None of the things that make their riches did they bring with them from beyond the Great Water; all comes from my land, the land the Great Mystery gave unto the Indian.

And when I think upon this I know that it is right, even thus. In the heart of the great Mystery it was meant that stranger-visitors—my friends across the Great Water—should sit down with me and eat together of my corn. It was meant by the Great Mystery that the Indian should give to all peoples.

But the white man never has known the Indian. It is thus: there are two roads, the white man's road, and the Indian's road. Neither traveller knows the road of the other. Thus ever has it been, from the long ago, even unto to-day. May this book help make the Indian truly known in the time to come.

The words of Hiamovi (High Chief) reflect the lack of materialism in the Native American culture, the willingness to share with those in need. Although he refers to some of the conflicts with the European settlers, he in no way mentions the influences that were most damaging to the Indian people.

When the first Europeans arrived, there were an estimated 90 to 112 million Native Americans living in the Western Hemisphere; 10 to 12 million of these were north of the Rio Grande, and 2.5 million were in what was to become the United States. By 1890 the American Indian population in the United States had declined to 250 thousand—a 90 percent reduction in 300 years. What caused this drastic decline? There were three major factors: disease, disruption of traditional life styles, and displacement.

The Cherokee Nation

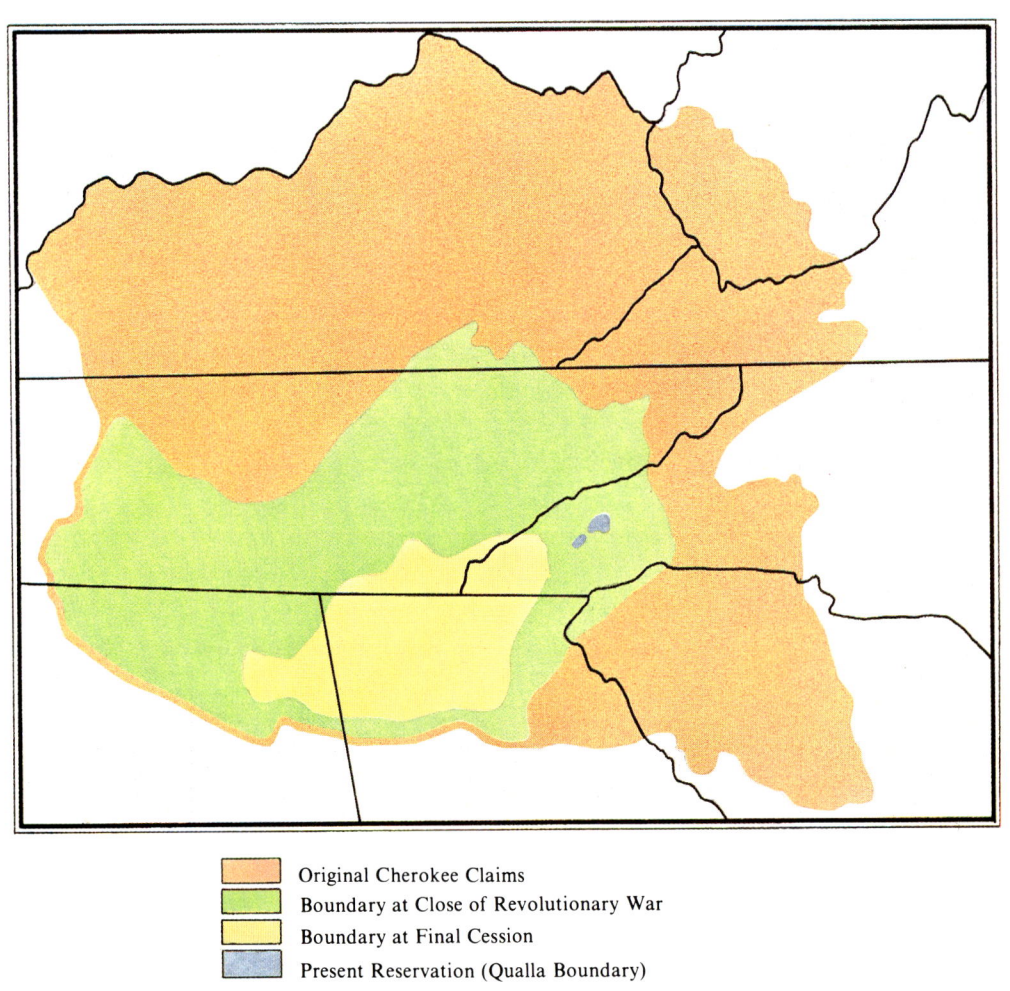

- Original Cherokee Claims
- Boundary at Close of Revolutionary War
- Boundary at Final Cession
- Present Reservation (Qualla Boundary)

The Europeans brought with them diseases for which the Indians, having been separated from Eurasian illnesses for more than twenty thousand years, had no natural immunity. Smallpox, measles, bubonic plague, and cholera killed thousands upon thousands of Indians. Some tribes died out completely before the first white man ever reached them. Effects of the strange new illnesses were sometimes made worse because the shaman used the traditional sweathouse treatment to drive out the evil spirits.

At first the European trade goods seemed to make life easier for the Native Americans. They could trade readily available animal skins for cloth, metal knives, and other goods they could not make. One of the most coveted items was the gun, which allowed the hunter to obtain many more skins for trading. After a while, the deer and other animals became scarce. The Indians did not have enough skins to settle their accounts with the traders, who often cheated by giving very little in return for the valuable pelts. Wanting more goods, a few men took some very bad advice from the traders: Raid one of the other tribes and bring captives for us to sell as slaves. This caused many tribal conflicts, disrupted farming and family life, and contributed to the number of deaths from malnutrition. Alcoholic beverages supplied by the traders also caused many problems for the Indians, who had never before had a year-round source of fermented drinks. Also, as inevitably happens when two cultures meet, many Native Americans married white settlers and adopted a new way of life.

Indian settlements, often strategically situated along waterways, were quickly replaced with cities built by the European invaders: Mexico City, Jamestown in Virginia, Plymouth and Boston in Massachusetts, New York City, Detroit, Chicago, Quebec, and Montreal were among the earliest of many such sites. Cahokia, America's first metropolis north of the Rio Grande, supported a population of thirty thousand Indians between AD 1100 and 1200. It was abandoned before the arrival of European settlers, probably because there was no longer enough firewood available within a reasonable distance from the city. Although most of this city now lies under modern development, its largest structure still stands in Cahokia Mounds State Park near East St. Louis, Illinois. This hundred-foot-tall, flat-topped mound has a sixteen-acre, rectangular base, which is larger than that of Egypt's Great Pyramid.

At first the Indians tried to accommodate the Europeans and later tried to drive them out. Neither strategy worked to the Native Americans' advantage. The white man was technologically superior, and his greed for land could not be satisfied. Treaty after treaty was broken as most of the Indians were pushed west of the Appalachian Mountains before 1700. But the Cherokees stubbornly remained in the southern Appalachians into the 1800s. On May 23, 1836, the United States Senate ratified the Treaty of New Echota, and President Andrew Jackson signed it. This document provided for moving the Cherokees to Oklahoma and Arkansas. After two years, only two thousand people had moved voluntarily. Under armed military guard the remaining Cherokees, along with their white spouses and black slaves, were rounded up and forced to go west by wagon train. Their route became known as "The Trail of Tears." On one five-month, midwinter trek, a group of twelve thousand Cherokees traveled in units of one thousand. Approximately four thousand men, women, and children died along the way. The people who survived the ordeal became the Western Band of the Cherokee Nation. Those who managed to elude the soldiers by hiding in the Appalachian Mountains became the Eastern Band. The outdoor drama *Unto These Hills* portrays the experiences of the Cherokee people during that difficult time.

Living by choice in rural, predominantly Indian communities or confined to reservations until recent years, Indians did not receive full United States citizenship until 1924 and could not vote until 1948. Nonetheless, Native Americans have defended this country in every war fought since its founding. One of the four U.S. Marines commemorated in the statue of the flag being raised on Iwo Jima in World War II is an American Indian.

According to the 1980 census, there are 1.4 million Native Americans living in the United States, and nearly 65 thousand of these are in North Carolina, which has the largest Indian population east of the Mississippi River. Millions of other people with Native American ancestors live among us. Some are totally unaware of the Indian in the family tree. Others take pride in claiming an Indian great-great-great grandparent.

The contributions of Native Americans have become so much a part of the American way of life that we rarely think of their Indian origins. Our maps are dotted with Indian names: *Manteo, Wanchese, Roanoke* Island, Cape *Hatteras, Pamlico* County, *Core* Banks, *Croatan* National Forest,

A Cherokee woman wearing a traditional dress shows an example of her finger weaving to a Native American man in modern attire. At powwows Indian people sing and dance in time-honored ways, exhibit and sell their handcrafts, and seek to strenghten family ties and tribal unity through the preservation of their heritage.

Neuse River, *Chowan* River, *Catawba* River, Lake *Waccamaw*, and *Nantahala* National Forest. The thunderbird, symbol of happiness, is widely used in jewelry making, fine arts, and advertising, notably in the name of a popular automobile. Sports fans root for teams bearing names of Indian tribes, and rock stars have Mohawk haircuts. Cowboys and rodeo riders wear chaps, a variation of the Indians' leather leggings. Quilters use the Seminole patchwork technique or mola, a reverse applique developed by the San Blas Indians of Panama; textile designers adapt ancient Indian symbols to modern fabrics; and swags of Indian corn hang by doorways each autumn. Jack-o-lanterns are carved from pumpkins, and this big, orange fruit turns up in fairy tales and nursery rhymes as well as on the Thanksgiving menu. We take aspirin, chew gum, hang martin gourds, and wear moccasins and ponchos. We eat succotash, chili, cornbread, and many other foods first prepared by American Indians. And what would we do without that all-American favorite—popcorn?

Native Americans excel in every field of endeavor—science, engineering, medicine, law, education, business, politics, religion, fine arts, athletics, and entertainment. Their accomplishments are not thought of as being particularly Indian because in their daily lives they look and act like all the other people doing the same kind of work. They wear everything from jeans to pressurized flight suits. They drive cars, fish from motor boats, and live in houses with all the modern conveniences they can afford. They enjoy the same sports and entertainment as their non-Indian neighbors. They worship in the same churches.

On special occasions, however, Native Americans dress in traditional clothing to sing and dance in time-honored ways. At these powwows, Indian people exhibit and sell their handmade beadwork, pottery, weavings, and other handiwork, and seek to strengthen family and tribal unity through the preservation of their heritage. Indian leaders counsel young Native Americans to take advantage of the opportunities available in modern American society but to do so within the context of their traditional Indian culture. The result is often a unique blend of the best of both worlds.

In proclaiming 1986 as the Year of the Native American in North Carolina, Governor James G. Martin noted the special ways Indians have contributed to the social, economic, and agricultural progress of the state and its people. He called upon all citizens to recognize and honor the past and present contributions of North Carolina's Native Americans.

Indian people now serve at every level of state and national government. They help run the nation that was founded in part on the democratic principles their ancestors tested long before the first European settlers arrived in America.

In the words of Haimovi:

*"There are birds
of many colors— red,
blue, green, yellow—yet it
is all one bird. There are horses of
many colors—brown, black, yellow, white
—yet it is all one horse. So cattle, so all living
things—animals, flowers, trees. So men: in this land
where once were only Indians are now men of
every color—white, black, yellow, red—
yet all one people. That this should
come to pass was in the heart of
the Great Mystery. It is right
thus. And everywhere
there shall be
peace."*

Places to Visit in North Carolina

Belhaven: A reconstruction of a Late Woodland stockaded village (assumed to represent the village of Aquascogoe, which was burned by Grenville's men in 1585) is modeled after the John White watercolor of the village of Pomeiooc. A small museum offers related displays.

Catawba Science Center: Hickory. Indian exhibit.

Charlotte Nature Museum: This Charlotte museum maintains collections of prehistoric and historic Indian materials and provides programs about Indians.

Cherokee: Situated in eastern Swain County and in the Qualla Boundary (Eastern Cherokee Indian Reservation), this town offers visitors many opportunities to learn about Native American life: the Museum of the Cherokee Indian, the Qualla Craft Shop, and the Oconaluftee Indian Village, a living museum where Native Americans demonstrate the arts and crafts of their ancestors. Each summer since 1950, the outdoor drama *Unto These Hills* has been produced here. It tells the tragic story of the forced removal of the Cherokees from the southern Appalachian Mountains in the 1830s.

Cherokee County Historical Museum, Inc.: Peachtree Street, Murphy. Indian artifacts on display.

Duke University Museum of Art: Durham. Pre-Columbian art, Peruvian textiles, and Navajo rugs on display.

Fort Cherokee Trading Post: Wilmington. Indian artifacts and relics.

Fort Raleigh National Historic Site: Near Manteo. Indian artifacts are displayed along with relics from the period of the first English colony in America. Outdoor drama, *The Lost Colony*, is presented in the summer.

Greensboro Historical Museum: 220 Church Street, Greensboro. Extensive displays of Indian and pioneer relics.

Indian Museum of the Carolinas: Laurinburg. Extensive displays of regional Indian artifacts.

Judacullah Rock: Situated on Caney Creek in central Jackson County, 3.5 miles southeast of East Laport, this large soapstone rock is covered with well-preserved Indian picture writing that apparently predates the arrival of the Cherokees. According to one legend, a giant named Tsulkalu used the rock as a stepping stone from his mountain home to a river. Recognizable objects include a river and a beaver.

Morrow Mountain State Park: In addition to various recreational facilities, this park in eastern Stanly County offers visitors an opportunity to tour a Natural History Museum and to see a site where American Indians obtained rock for projectile points.

Museum of Man: Wake Forest University, 114 Reynolda Village, Winston-Salem. Exhibits include Indian artifacts from North and South America.

Museum of Natural History: Highlands. Cherokee artifacts.

Museum of the Albemarle: Elizabeth City. Indian exhibit.

Museum of the American Indian: Blowing Rock Road, Boone.
Native American Library: This Pembroke library houses the Lumbee Regional Development Association's collection of books and audio-visual aids pertaining to American Indians.
Native American Resource Center: Pembroke State University, College Road, Pembroke. Housed in historic Old Main Building on the campus of the first four-year liberal arts college established specifically for American Indians, the center preserves substantial collections of Native American arts and crafts. Handcrafted Lumbee Indian baskets and jewelry are offered for sale along with books about Indians.
North Carolina Museum of Art: Blue Ridge Blvd., Raleigh. Pre-Columbian art.
North Carolina Museum of History: In the state government complex in downtown Raleigh, this museum has extensive collections of North Carolina American Indian artifacts, only a small portion of which can be displayed at any one time. Copies of John White's drawings are on exhibit. Books about American Indians are for sale.
North Carolina Museum of Life and Science: This Durham museum has collections of Indian artifacts and offers summer classes in Indian lore.
North Carolina State Museum of Natural Sciences: In the state government complex in downtown Raleigh, this museum displays mounted specimens of many of the animals Indians hunted. Programs about Native Americans, their arts and crafts, and the natural world in which they lived are available. Books about American Indians are for sale.
Pembroke: *Strike at the Wind*, the story of Henry Berry Lowrie and the Lumbee Indians, is a summer outdoor drama. See also, Native American Library and Native American Resource Center.
Roanoke Island Historical Park: Manteo, open May through September. The Roanoke Indian Village is a reconstruction of a coastal Algonquian village at the time of European contact. A living museum offers demonstrations of dances, crafts, and Indian technology. Powwows are held on Tuesday and Thursday evenings.
Rowan Museum, Inc.: 114 S. Jackson Street, Salisbury. Indian exhibits.
Schiele Museum of Natural History and Planetarium, Inc.: 1500 E. Garrison Blvd., Gastonia. Collections include American Indian arts, crafts, costumes, and tools. There are dioramas and other displays of Indian materials. A major project is the excavation and restoration of an Indian village. Many programs about Native Americans are sponsored by the museum.
Town Creek Indian Mound: This 53-acre state historic site was established in 1937 near Mount Gilead in southern Montgomery County. In addition to a museum, there is an excavated and restored Indian ceremonial center.
Wachovia Museum: Winston-Salem. Located in Old Salem, this museum has a collection of American Indian relics.

Sources and Suggested Reading

America 1585. The Complete Drawings of John White. John Hulton. University of North Carolina Press, Chapel Hill, 1984.

The American Indian in North Carolina. Douglas L. Rights. Blair Publishers, Winston-Salem, 1957.

Cherokee Plants and Their Uses. Paul B. Hamel and Mary Ulmer Chiltoskey. Herald Publishing Co., Sylva, N.C., 1975.

The Cherokees Past and Present: An Authentic Guide to the Cherokee People. J. Ed Sharpe. Cherokee Publications, Cherokee, N.C., 1970.

"Digging Up The Distant Past." Mark Taylor. *Wildlife in North Carolina*, August 1986.

The Early Indians. Charles Parel May. Thomas Nelson, Inc., New York, 1971.

First on the Land: The North Carolina Indians. Ruth Y. Wetmore. John F. Blair, Winston-Salem, 1975.

Frontiers in the Soil: The Archaeology of Georgia. Roy S. Dickens, Jr., and James L. McKinley. Frontier Publishing Co., P.O. Box 963, Chapel Hill, N.C., 27514, 1979.

"A Historical Perspective about the Indians of North Carolina and an Overview of the Commission of Indian Affairs." N.C. Com. Indian Affairs. *N.C. Historical Review* LVI(2):177-187, 1979.

"How the Indians Hunted & Fished." Tom Taylor. *Wildlife in North Carolina*, February 1981.

The Indian How Book. Arthur C. Parker. Unabridged republication, Dover Publishing Co., New York, 1931 edition.

Indians of North America. Geoffrey Turner. Blandford Press, Dorset, U.K., 1979.

The Iroquois and the Founding of the American Nation. Donald A. Grinde, Jr. Indian Historian Press, San Francisco, 1977.

Man Comes to the New World. Harold Coy. Little Brown, Boston, 1973.

Native Carolinians: The Indians of North Carolina. Theda Perdue. N.C. Dept. Cultural Resources, Raleigh, 1985.

Native Tribal Arts and Traditions: A Cultural Crafts Manual of the American Indian of the Southeast and Other Areas. Arnold Richardson. Haliwa-Saponi Culture Group, Hollister, N.C., 1981; reprinted by Durham Technical Institute, 1986.

North American Indian Arts. Andrew Hunter Whiteford. Golden Guide Series, Golden Press, New York, 1983.

North Carolina Indians. N.C. Com. Indian Affairs, P.O. Box 27228, Raleigh, N.C. 27611, 1985.

North Carolina Marine Education Manual, Unit Four: Coastal Beginnings. Lundie Mauldin and Dirk Frankenberg, editors. Sea Grant Publication UNC-SG 78-14-E, Raleigh, 1979.

"North Carolina Prehistory, Part Two: The Paleo-Indians." Stephen R. Claggett. *Friends of North Carolina Archaeology, Inc., Newsletter*, Spring 1985.

The Only Land I Know: A History of the Lumbee Indians. Adolph L. Dial and David K. Eliades. Indian Historian Press, San Francisco, 1975.

The Prehistory of North Carolina: An Archaeological Symposium. Mark A. Mathis and Jeffrey J. Crow, editors. N.C. Div. Archives and History, Raleigh, 1983.

"The Role of the Indian in North Carolina History." Ruth Y. Wetmore. *N.C. Historical Review* LVI(2):162-176, 1979.

"The Search for the First Americans." Thomas Y. Canby. *National Geographic*, September 1979.

Set Fair for Roanoke: Voyages and Colonies, 1584-1616. David Beers Quinn. University of North Carolina Press, Chapel Hill, 1985.

Southern Indian Myths and Legends. Virginia Brown and Laurella Owens. Beechwood Books, Birmingham, Ala., 1984.

Sun Circles and Human Hands. Emma Lila Fundaburk and Mary Douglass Fundaburk Foreman. Luverne, Ala., 1957.

"Who Were the 'Mound Builders'?" George E. Stuart. *National Geographic*, December 1972.

The World of the Southern Indian. Virginia Brown and Laurella Owens. Beechwood Books, Birmingham, Ala., 1984.

SLIDE SHOW

The Carolina Algonkians: Archaeology and History. David S. Phelps. East Carolina University, Greenville, 1984. Distributed by N.C. Div. Archives and History, Archaeology Branch, 507 N. Blount Street, Raleigh, N.C. 27601.

ARCHAEOLOGY SUPPORT GROUP

Friends of North Carolina Archaeology, Inc., 109 E. Jones Street, Raleigh, N.C. 27611. *Newsletter* offers reports on recent discoveries, book reviews, and original articles of interest to amateur archaeologists and general readers.

Native American Organizations

Federal Government

U.S. Bureau of Indian Affairs
18th and E Streets N.W.
Washington, DC 20245

North Carolina State Government

Commission of Indian Affairs
227 E. Edenton Street
P.O. Box 27228
Raleigh, NC 27611

Division of Indian Education
N.C. Department of Public Instruction
100 W. Edenton Street
Raleigh, NC 27601

North Carolina Tribal Councils and Native American Associations

Coharie Intra-Tribal Council
Route 3, Box 340-E
Clinton, NC 28328

Cumberland County Association
  for Indian People
102 Indian Drive
Fayetteville, NC 28301

Eastern Band of the Cherokee
P.O. Box 455
Cherokee, NC 28719

Guilford Native American Association
P.O. Box 5623
Greensboro, NC 27403

Haliwa-Saponi Indian Tribe
P.O. Box 99
Hollister, NC 27844

Harnett County Indian Association
Route 4, Box 299
Dunn, NC 28334

Lumbee Regional Development
  Association
P.O. Box 68
Pembroke, NC 28372

Meherrin Tribe
P.O. Box 508
Winton, NC 27986

Metrolina Native American Association
Mart Office Building - Suite CC-513
900 Briar Creek Road, Charlotte, NC 28205

Triangle Native American Society
4708 Pearl Road
Raleigh, NC 27610

Waccamaw-Siouan Development Association
P.O. Box 221
Bolton, NC 28423

Newspapers

Carolina Indian Voice
College Plaza
P.O. Box 1075
Pembroke, NC 28372

Cherokee One Feather
Acquoni Road
P.O. Box 501
Cherokee, NC 28719

Index

A
adobe, 36
adz, 58-59
agriculture, Algonquian, 45, 47, 59-60
    early, 24, 27, 29, 30, 43
    Indian contributions to, 27, 72
    support of cities, 37, 43-44
Albany Conference, 36
Aleuts, 37
Algonquians, 43, 44, 45-65
    reconstructed village, 74, 75
    slide show about, 77
animals, domesticated, 26, 27, 30, 46
    extinct, 15-17, 20-22, 39
    game, 15, 16, 22, 24, 39, 43, 57
    reptiles and amphibians, 13, 24, 51, 59
    use of, 18
    see also, mammals, names of animals
antler, 56-57, 64
Aquascogoe, 74
archaeology, 15, 30, 77
Archaic Period, 24, 43
armor, wooden, 33
arrowheads, 32-33, 56-57
art, Indian, 28, 29, 30, 74, 75
atlatl, 23, 25
awl, 51
axe, 18, 33, 43, 46
Aztec, 29, 30, 36

B
bannerstone, 23, 25
baskets, 16, 18, 24, 39, 43
bear, 15, 43, 57, 60
    grease, use of, 57, 60
    short-faced, 16-17
beaver, 16-17, 22
bee, honey, 62
Bering Strait, 13-16, 19, 27
    land bridge, 14-15
beverages, 55, 59, 69
birds, 13, 60
    effigies of, 48
    in legends, 65
    Passenger Pigeon, 57, 62
    Purple Martin, 60
    turkey, 27, 52, 57
    waterfowl, 27, 57
    see also, feathers
bison, 15, 16-17, 21, 22, 27, 39
blowgun, 57
boats, reed, 29; *see also,* canoe
books, accordion-folded, 29
bow and arrow, 43, 57, 64
buckskin, 49, 50-51, 64
buffalo, *see* bison
buildings, 36-37, 46-48, 60
    council house/lodge, 34, **43**, 46, 55
    huts, 37, 43, 44
    longhouse, 37, 46-48, 60-61
    plank houses, 36-37
    pueblos, 36-37
    temples, 30, 46
    see also, mounds, shelters
burial customs, 46

C
calendars, 29, 30
calumet, 34
camel, 13, 16-17, 22, 27
campsites, 18, 19, 23, 24
canoes, 23, 26-27, 38, 45, 57, 58-59
Cape Fear Indians, 44
Catawba Indians, 44
Cayuga Indians, 34
celts, 44
chaps, 72
Cheraw Indians, 44
Cherokee, 31, 44, 52, 57, 70, 71, 74
    Eastern Band of the, 70, 74, 78
    Nation, 34, 68
    Western Band of the, 70
children, 27, 48, 49, 57, 59, 62, 64, 65, 70
chocolate, 27
cities, Indian, 29, 30, 37, 69
cloth, carrying, 28
clothing, 18, 28, 38, 49-52, 70-71, 72
Coharie Indians, 78
Columbus, Christopher, 36, 38
competitions, 19, 31
cooking, 18, 39, 60
    utensils, 23, 39, 42-43, 62
    see also, baskets
copper, 29, 34, 38, 44, 48, 52
Coree Indians, 44
corn, 24, 27, 47, 60
    Indian, 27, 72
    popcorn, 72
cornbread, 60, 72
cornmeal making, 60-61
cotton, 27, 29, 30
cradle board, use of, 62
Creek Indians, 31

D
dancing, 49 (illus), 65
deer, 15, 43, 57, 69
    giant, 16-17
    hide, tanning, 51
    white-tail, 43, 57, 64
Dekanawida, 34
democracy, 36, 72
disease, 30, 68, 69
dog, 26-27, 46
drill, 18
dyes, 27

E
effigies, 28, 29, 48, 53
Enlightenment movement, 35
Eno Indians, 44
Eskimos, 16, 36, 43
Europeans, 33, 34, 38, 39, 43, 62, 68, 69, 70, 72
    English, 44, 49, 52, 74
    explorers, 36-39, 41, 44, 48, 64, 74, 75
    Spanish, 30

F
family life, Indian, 33, 48, 57, 59, 62, 64, 72
feathers, use of, 48, 52, 54-55
festivals, 47, 55
fire, 18, 36, 39, 60
    ceremonial, 53
    in canoe making, 59
    in felling trees, 58
    in fishing, 58
    in habitat management, 57
    in hunting, 57
    pit, 43
firewood, 45, 62, 69
fishing, 18, 19, 45, 57, 58
flute, courting, 48
fluting, in spear points, 21
food gathering, 16, 23, 24, 43, 59
foods, 16, 18, 24, 27, 59, 60, 62
    cultivated, 24, 27, 60, 72
    see also, corn
forests, 22, 23, 37, 39, 43
    management of, 57
Franklin, Benjamin, 35
furniture, 48

G
gold, 29, 30
gourds, 24, 60, 65, 72
government, 33-36, 48
Green Corn Ceremony, 47, 55
gum, chewing, 27, 72
guns, trading for, 69

H
hair, care of, 57
    styles, 52-53
Haliwa-Saponi Indians, 78
Hiamovi, 67, 73
Hiawatha, 34
homes, *see* buildings, shelters, villages
Hopewell Period, 34, 43
horse, 13, 15, 16-17, 22, 27, 30
hunting, 16, 43, 45, 57
    bands (clans), 16, 19
    mammoth, 20-21
    sea mammals, 37
    use of fire in, 57
    with bow and arrow, 43, 57
    with decoys, 57
    with net, 16
    with spear thrower, 23, 25, 43
    see also, weapons

I-J-K
Ice Age, 13-16, 18
    end of, 22, 23, 27, 39
    megafauna, 16-17
Inca, 28, 29, 30
Indians, American, citizenship of, 70
    language groups, N.C., 40, 44
    origin of name, 38
    physical characteristics of, 16, 19, 44
    population, 68, 70
        N.C., 40, 70
    role in modern U.S. life, 70, 72
    tribal organizations, N.C., 78
    tribes, N.C., 1580s, 40-41, 44
    see also, Archaic Period, Paleo-Indians, Plains Indians, tribal names, Woodland Indians, Woodland Period
Iroquois, 33, 34, 35, 36, 37
Jefferson, Thomas, 35, 36
Judacullah Rock, 74

Keyauwee Indians, 44
knives, 18, 69

L
lacrosse, 31
languages, Indian, 16, 21, 40, 41, 44, 65
    Mobilian, 44
    sign, 33, 44
    use in place names, 45, 70, 72
legends, 62, 65, 74
llama, 15, 26-27
Lowrie, Henry Berry, 75
Lumbee Indians, 75, 78

M
maize, *see* corn
mammals, 13, 15, 16, 22, 24, 37, 39, 43, 57, 60
mammoth, 15, 16-17, 20-22
man, primitive, 15-16

Manteo, 70, 75
marriage, Indian customs, 48, 64
    to European settlers, 69, 70
Martin, James G., 72
mastodon, 15, 16-17, 39
Maya, 29
medicine man, *see* shaman
medicines, 27, 55, 72
Meherrin Indians, 44, 78
metalworking, 29
mica, 34, 35
microliths, 43
moccasins, 51, 52, 72
Mohawk, 34, 36
    hair style, 52, 72
mola, 72
Morrow Mountain State Park, 74
mounds, pryamidal, 29, 30, 31, 43, 69
    Aztec, 30
    Cahokia, 69
    Town Creek, 31
Mountains, Andes, 19, 27
    Appalachian, 19, 31, 39, 70
    Rocky, 14, 19
    Sandia, 21
music, instruments for making
    bells, 52, 65
    drum, 65
    flute, 48
    rattles, 65
musk-ox, 15, 22

N
Native American, museum exhibits, 74, 75
    newspapers, 78
    organizations, 78
    Year of the, 72
Navajo rugs, 74
needles, sewing, 18, 39, 51
North Carolina, 21, 24, 31, 34, 39-65, 72, 74-75, 78

O
obsidian, 34
Occaneechi Indians, 44
Old Hendrick, 36
Oneida Indians, 34
Onondaga Indians, 34
ornaments, 18, 48, 49, 52-53
ossuaries, 46

P
Paleo-Indians, 14, 16, 19, 21, 22, 39
Panama, 19, 72
paper, 29
peace making, 34
Pembroke, 75
    State University, 75
Peru, 28, 29, 74
pipes, 34, 53
Plains Indians, 22, 51, 52
Pomeiooc, 46-47, 74
porcupine quills, 34, 51, 52
pottery, 29, 43, 44, 62-63
Powhatan, 44
powwow, 70, 72, 75
priests, Algonquian, 48, 53
Pueblo Indians, 36
pyramids, 29, 30

Q
Qualla Boundary, 68, 74
quipu, 29, 34, 35

R
rabbits, 16, 24, 53, 57
raccoons, 60
religion, freedom of, 36
    Roman Catholic, 30
    Native American, 30, 33, 48, 53, 55, 72
River, Amazon, 36
    Mackenzie, 15
    Mississippi, 31, 70
    Missouri, 15
    Ohio, 15, 34, 43
    Pee Dee, 31
    Rio Grande, 68, 69
roach, 52
roadways, paved, 29
Roanoke Island, 39, 44, 70, 75
rosin, use of, 59
rubber, 27

S
sachem, 48
San Blas Indians, 72
sandals, yucca fiber, 24
Saponi Indians, 44, 78
scrapers, 18, 50-51
Seminole patchwork, 72
Seneca Indians, 34
Shakori Indians, 44
shaman, 48, 54-55, 69
shellfish, 18, 59
shells, 34, 62
    as ornaments, 52
    quahog, 34, 59
    use in wampum, 34
shelters, cliff/lean-to, 39
silver, 29, 30
sinew, 18, 42-43, 51
Sissipahaw Indians, 44
skin care, 52, 57
    decoration, 48, 49
slaves, 33, 36, 60, 69, 70
sleds, 27
soapstone, 23, 42-43, 74
spear, fishing, 57, 58
    points, 18, 21
    shaft, 18
    thrower, 23, 25, 43
stone, boiling, 18, 39
    carving, 29, 42-43, 74
    for weapons, 21, 57
    grinding, 18, 39
    milling, 23, 60-61
    nutting, 23
    see also, tools
Sugaree Indians, 44
sweathouse, 55, 69

T
tattoos, 48, 49
tepee, 37
teeth, human, 16, 24
    animal, 52
textiles, 28; *see also*, clothing, weaving
thanksgiving festivals, 55
thunderbird, 72
tobacco, 24, 53, 60
tomahawk, 34; *see also*, axe
tools, 15, 18, 23, 39, 42-43, 44, 46, 51, 57, 59-60, 61, 64
    use in farming, 60
    see also, knives, stone, weapons
totems, 36
Town Creek Indian Mound, 31, 75

trade, 27, 37, 38
    leagues to promote, 34
    with European settlers, 69
Trail of Tears, 70
travois, 26-27
trees, 22
    birch, 59, 62
    cedar, white, 59
    coniferous, 22, 39
    cypress, 58
    deciduous, 39
    hardwood, 22
    maple, 22, 62
    oak, 22
    pine, 22
    poplar, 58
    sugar maple, 62
    sweet birch, 62
    willow, 48
    see also, forests
Tuscarora Indians, 34, 44
Tutelo Indians, 44

U-V
United States, 14, 15, 22, 30
    citizenship, Indian, 70
    Constitution, 36
    Indian population of, 68
    treaties with Indians, 70

vanilla, 27
villages, Algonquian, 45, 46, 47, 57, 75
    reconstructed, 74, 75

W
Waccamaw Indians, 44, 78
wampum (wampumpeage), 34, 35
war bonnet, 52
war, little brother of, 31
War, Revolutionary, 33, 34
    World, II, 70
warfare, 19, 33
Washington, George, 33
Wateree Indians, 44
Waxhaw Indians, 44
weapons, 18, 21, 23, 24-25, 32-33, 43, 56-57, 64
    see also, gun
weaving, 28, 29, 30
    finger, 51, 70-71
    mats, 48, 62
weir, 53, 57
wheel, 27
White, John, 39, 41, 44, 74, 75
    drawings by, 46, 47, 58
Woccon Indians, 44
wolves, 15, 16-17
women, Indian, 24, 43, 48, 49, 52, 57, 59-62, 65
Woodland Indians (Eastern), 22, 31, 33, 51, 59, 74
Woodland Period, 43
writing, 29, 74

Y
yaupon, tea made from, 55
Yellowstone National Park, 34

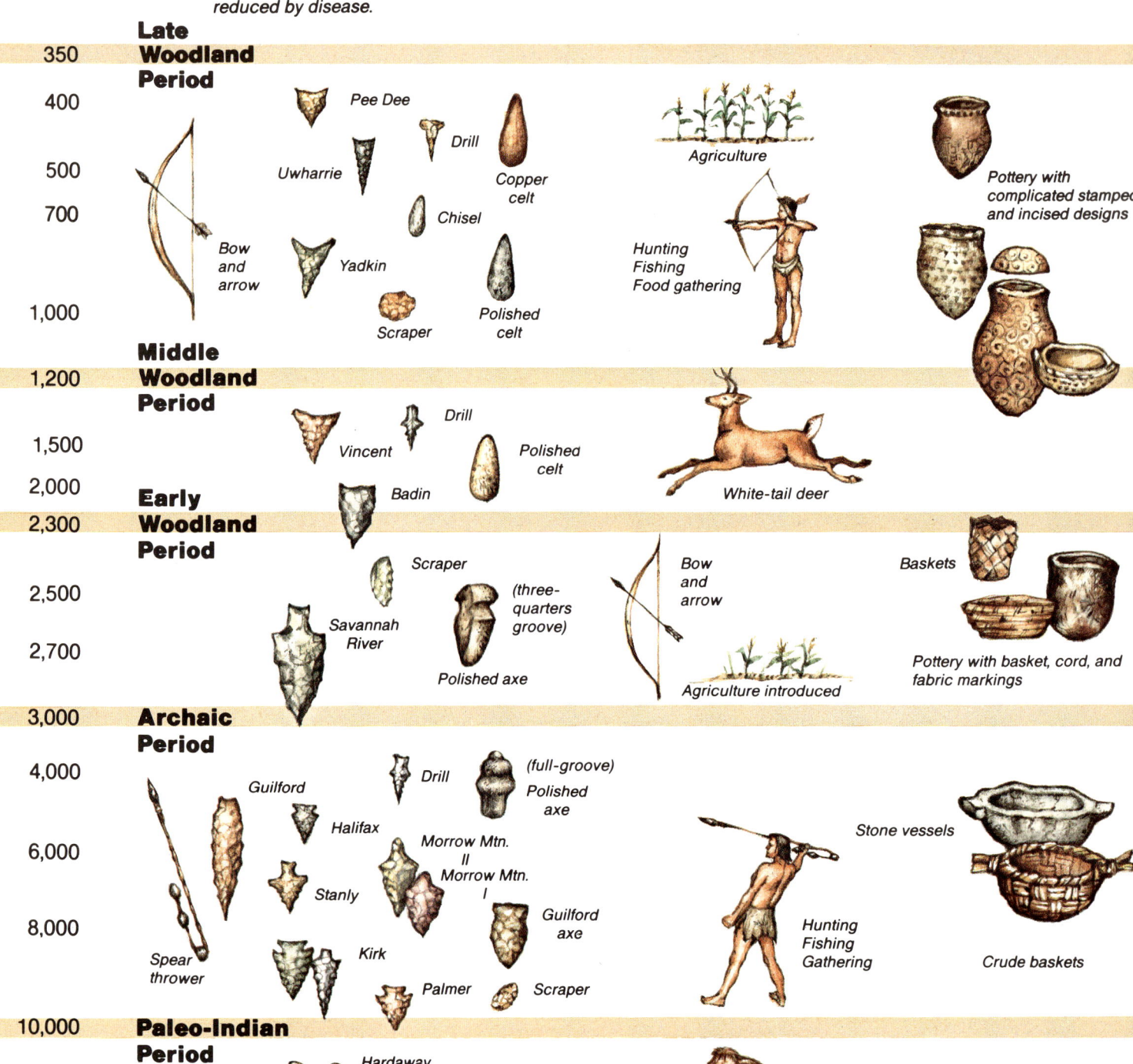